Famous

FANTASY CHARACTER MONOLOGS

Starring the Not-So-Wicked Witch and more

REBECCA YOUNG

MERIWETHER PUBLISHING LTD.
Colorado Springs, Colorado

Meriwether Publishing Ltd., Publisher
PO Box 7710
Colorado Springs, CO 80933-7710

Editor: Arthur L. Zapel
Assistant editor: Audrey Scheck
Cover design: Jan Melvin

Library of Congress Cataloging-in-Publication Data

Young, Rebecca, 1965-
    Famous fantasy character monologs starring the not-so-wicked witch
    and more / by Rebecca Young.
        p. cm.
    ISBN-13: 978-1-56608-116-0
    ISBN-10: 1-56608-116-5
    1. Monologues, American. 2. Characters and characteristics—Drama. I. Title.
    PS3625.O969F36 2006
    812'.04508—dc22
                            2006017338

1   2   3   06   07   08

Dedication

To Marcia Jones for her inspiration and advice — I couldn't have made it through the last few monologs without her; my mom for her careful edits; Dennis for being my informal "publicist"; and Keith, Donald, and MaryAnne for cheering me on; the rest of the family for their love and support; my daughters (Heather, Kristina, and Ashley Gritton) for being the ultimate drama queens; my editor, Art Zapel, for believing in me; Audrey Scheck for her great attitude and efficiency (how do you get the answers so fast?); my great friend Sandi Froehlich who listens to my drama woes; and my husband Frank for doing the laundry so I can write! You guys are the best!

CONTENTS

Section 2: Monologs for Guys .... .69

About the Author

INTRODUCTION:
The Not-So-Wicked Witch

You know, you really shouldn't believe everything you hear. It'll get you into trouble every time. Remember when you played that game where you whisper a secret in someone's ear, and then they whisper it into someone else's ear, and you keep passing the secret around the room? You never got the same secret at the end, did you? Instead of everyone hearing that "You love Roy," it came out that "You want to be a boy," or something else totally horrifying!

Well, it's the same thing with stories. They get retold so much that by the time someone writes them down, there isn't anything but half-truths hidden within them. They become a pack of lies, twisted and turned until nobody could straighten out the real story from what's left.

Take me, for instance. I've got a story to tell. I do. But nobody wants to hear it. Instead they listen to Little Miss Good Witch, who has obviously cast a spell over everyone. Somehow she made the whole world believe she's so sweet, sugar wouldn't melt in her mouth.

Well, just like I'm not so wicked, she's not so good. She's messed up a time or two. Cast a bad spell. Brewed a rotten potion. Just never gets caught. But who you gonna believe? Someone dressed in black? Yeah, right. It's a bum rap I've had all these years.

All I ask is that you take time to hear how things really happened. To me and to others. Oh, don't look so shocked. I'm not the only one. You'll see — there are plenty more like me: Other characters with a story to tell, living lives of twisted truths. Read on and find out what really happened.

Love,

The Not-So-Wicked Witch

PREFACE

Could it be? The Wicked Witch is really not so wicked? The Boogeyman is scared of the dark? The Tooth Fairy hates her job? What would these characters say if they really had a chance to talk to you? Find out firsthand in *Famous Fantasy Character Monologs*. Hear the side of the story you've been missing since the day your mother read you your first fairy tale!

You will recognize the fantasy characters in this collection of monologs even though the names have been changed to fit the style of a parody presentation. The monologs are short, easy to memorize, and perfect for school talent shows, drama classes, auditions, or even family reunions! With or without costumes, these monologs are sure to be a hit. Not only that … they're fun, too!

The variety of monologs here offers something for everyone. It's time to rev up those creative juices and jump into character. You'll be so glad you did!

Sincerely,

Rebecca Young,
the Not-So-Famous Author

SECTION 1

MONOLOGS FOR GIRLS

The Not-So-Wicked Witch

1   Everyone thinks my sister is perfect! It makes me want to
2 choke a toad! All pretty in pink like a big puff of cotton candy!
3 As if sugar wouldn't melt in her little rosebud mouth!

4   Well, duh, of course she looks all sweet and nice — she's
5 dressed all girly from her head to her toes! Nobody thinks evil
6 could reside in all that fluff!

7   It just proves that she's Mom and Dad's favorite. What do
8 they give *me* to wear? Black, black, and more black! How's a
9 person to look nice in that? And do you *know* how *hot* it gets
10 wearing black all summer long? It's no wonder I'm a bit
11 grouchy at times! Of course, she's all smiles and full of cute
12 little songs with her perky little voice! Well, let her wear this
13 get-up for a while and we'll see how she feels!

14   But not Glinda! Oh no! She's the Good Witch! So what
15 does that make me? The Bad One, of course. What a joke!
16 She's the one that turned all of the townspeople into
17 munchkins! And didn't even get in trouble. I turn one little guy
18 into a scarecrow, and all of a sudden I'm wicked. It's just not
19 fair! She gets away with everything.

20   It makes me so mad; I've just got to *zap* someone! *(Makes*
21 *pointing gesture to someone in audience.)*

22   *Zap*! *(Blows off zapping finger.)* **There. Now I do feel a little**
23 **better.**

Shopping-Compulsive Cinderella

1 I have a problem. I do. I see something I want and I *have*
2 to have it. Even if it's something completely ridiculous — like
3 glass shoes! I just love to shop, shop, shop. "Shop 'til you
4 drop" is even embroidered on my hankie. My stepsisters
5 thought it was funny, but it's true.

6 They try to keep me busy so I don't have time to shop, but
7 it doesn't work. While I'm scrubbing and cleaning, I'm
8 planning my trip to the store. I can hold a mental list of one
9 hundred items, no problem!

10 But my obsession is really getting out of hand. Take the
11 shoes again. I knew they were too big when I bought them. A
12 whole size at least. But I got them anyway. I mean, I couldn't
13 pass them up. They were perfect. So sparkly. Without a
14 doubt, they would look amazing with my ball gown.

15 And they did. You should've seen me. I looked like a
16 princess!

17 But man, did those sparkly little pieces of heaven hurt! I'd
18 only had one dance with the prince when the back of my heel
19 starting feeling like it was on fire! Now I have a huge blister.
20 One more reminder of why I should never have gotten those
21 shoes! Shoes made of glass? Whoever came up with such a
22 silly idea! I spent a whole month's allowance and now, since
23 I only have one, I can't even return them and get my money
24 back!

25 See, just as I was leaving the ball, my left shoe fell off. If
26 I had stopped to get it, I would've been left to walk home.
27 Walk home! With feet that could barely handle standing! Just
28 getting to the coach was agony!

29 I thought I'd spend the night dreaming about the

1   handsome prince, but all I could think about was my aching
2   feet! I had to soak them for hours. Now they're so swollen they
3   might actually fit in those oversized shoes! Too bad though,
4   because I'm never putting my tootsies anywhere near those
5   glass slippers ever again! Somebody's gotta help me stop
6   shopping! It's becoming a matter of life and death!

The Disgruntled Tooth Fairy

1   I am so tired! I spent all night flying around, and I'm
2 plumb worn out! Not to mention bruised! Doesn't anyone use
3 a nightlight anymore? I couldn't see a thing, and I must've
4 bumped into a dozen dressers! And for what? No one even
5 cares about me. Used to be, I'd get sweet little notes thanking
6 me for visiting. Some houses, I'd even get cookies. And
7 maybe a glass of milk. But those days are long gone.

8   Nowadays, if I do get a note, it's not to say thanks. Oooh,
9 nooo! It's to tell me exactly how much I'm supposed to pay
10 for a silly little white nub wrapped in bloody toilet paper! And
11 it's not cheap either! Kids these days want more and more!
12 I'm running out of money!

13   It used to be a fair trade; now I feel like I'm getting robbed!
14 A dollar? You've got to be kidding me! Who pays a dollar for
15 a tooth? I'm not rich, you know!

16   I don't know why I do this night after night. Maybe I
17 should move on. Be a fairy godmother or something. You
18 know, turn pumpkins into coaches! Now, that would be cool!

19   But then I think about all those children going to bed
20 every night, waiting for me. How would they feel if I just didn't
21 show up? Their little hearts would be broken. And what would
22 parents do with all those little teeth? Throw them away? Oh,
23 I couldn't let that happen!

24   Maybe I just need a nap ... and an ice pack, *(Holds*
25 *"bruised" leg)* and then I'll be flying around again in no time!

I'm Not a Sea Witch!
I'm Just on a Diet

1   I know I haven't been the nicest creature in the sea lately,
2 but do I really deserve to be called a witch? Ouch. That seems
3 kind of harsh. Especially after I've helped so many poor souls
4 get what they want.

5   Besides, who wouldn't be a little testy? For over two years,
6 I've been on a seafood — and I do mean *fish* — diet. Yeah, I've
7 heard all the jokes: Do you eat everything you *see*? Hilarious,
8 isn't it?

9   This stupid diet isn't even working. I've only eaten shrimp
10 or fish for breakfast, lunch, and dinner, and I'm as big as a
11 whale! Forced to hide away in this cave like I'm some kind of
12 criminal or something.

13   To top things off, I got this annoying mermaid who keeps
14 begging me for favors. Just the sight of her skinny scaled
15 body makes me want to vomit! What the heck does she *eat*
16 anyway? Pure water? Even that makes me fat — all that salt!
17 I retain water like a sponge. It's just not fair.

18   I can't win for losing. You'd think with all these arms I
19 could get some serious exercise in — but it doesn't matter
20 what I do; I don't lose a pound. At first I thought, "Cool.
21 Everyone knows muscle weighs more than fat." I figured I was
22 getting leaner and leaner. Then I went up top and caught my
23 reflection! *Flab City!* So much for water aerobics!

24   So, yeah. I'm a *little* grumpy. You might even say ...
25 witchy! But don't I deserve to be? You try choking down a
26 seaweed salad every night for dinner! *Without dressing*!

27   Well, I'm done with dieting. My new motto is: Big is
28 Beautiful. I tell you what, next ship that goes down, I'm eating
29 the whole pantry!

Sneaky Snow White

1   My stepmother hates me. She does! No matter what I do,
2 she's always yelling at me. All my life she's made me wear
3 ratty old clothes and has never ever bought me anything new.
4 I even have to use a comb that's missing half its teeth
5 because every time that witch would find me brushing my
6 hair, she'd take my brush! She's always telling me that I'm
7 ugly and that no prince in the land would ever look twice at
8 me!

9   I guess that's why I couldn't help but play a little joke on
10 her. It was so easy, too! She was always staring into this
11 mirror and talking to it like a crazy woman! "Mirror, mirror, on
12 the wall," she'd say, "who's the prettiest one of all?" Who in
13 their right mind talks to a mirror?

14   I know it wasn't right, but I just couldn't resist! I started
15 hiding behind the velvet drapes, and when she'd talk to the
16 mirror, I'd answer back. That very first time, you should've
17 seen her face! It was like she'd seen a ghost! Which is kind
18 of funny because she's always saying that I'm so pale I look
19 half-dead!

20   Anyway, from then on, every day she'd ask the mirror the
21 same thing, and every day I'd answer back. I always said that
22 she was the prettiest one in the land because I knew that's
23 what she wanted to hear. And, to be honest, I was hoping it'd
24 make her a little nicer. But it never did. If anything, she got
25 obsessed with the stupid mirror. So one night when she
26 asked, "Who's the prettiest?" I told her it was me. The dark-
27 haired beauty right under her nose.

28   She was so angry! She even broke the mirror! I could tell
29 that she wanted to kill me so that she could be the "prettiest

1   in the land" again. How could she even believe that? Hadn't

2   she ever looked in a *real* mirror? Well, I wanted to explain my

3   little joke to her, but I didn't think she'd listen, so I ran away.

4   Now I'm stuck living in the woods with these seven funny little

5   men. It's not bad, don't get me wrong. But it's not home. I tell

6   you the truth; I'll never impersonate another mirror for as long

7   as I live!

Dorothy the Ungrateful

1 Follow the yellow brick road, my foot! This thing never
2 ends! I've been skipping along for hours, and I think I'm going
3 in circles! I swear I've seen that scarecrow before! Why did I
4 ever get directions from a bunch of munchkins? I should've
5 known from all that giggling that they were up to something!

6 There's probably no such thing as a Wizard of Oz or an
7 Emerald City. If there was, and if it was as great as they said,
8 wouldn't someone have offered to go with me?

9 They just wanted to get rid of me. Get me as far away
10 from their little town as possible before that wicked witch
11 came back. Well, it wasn't my fault my house landed on her
12 stupid sister.

13 All I wanted was to go home. Couldn't Glinda just wave
14 that magic wand of hers and send me back to Kansas?

15 "Go to Oz," she said. "The Wizard will help you."

16 What was wrong with *her* helping me? After all, I landed
17 my house on their stupid old witch, didn't I? Didn't she owe
18 me a little something for that? And not a stupid pair of shoes,
19 either! I ask for help and instead I get some lame directions
20 and a pair of glittery red shoes that are at least a half size too
21 small! Now she's got me walking in circles in a pair of shoes
22 that are causing some very un-magical blisters! And they
23 won't come off! I've tried!

24 But now, to beat it all, I think I'm losing my mind because
25 I'm pretty sure that scarecrow over there just smiled at me!

26 Oh, Auntie Em! There's no place like home! There's no
27 place like home!

Goldilocks,
Crime Scene Investigator

1   I think something's happened to the family that lives here!
2 Something horrible. I was passing by when this wonderful
3 smell of fresh porridge filled my nose! When I peeked through
4 the windows — there they were! Three bowls, all different
5 sizes, full of porridge, and no one to be seen! Doesn't that
6 seem a little strange to you? Pour yourself a hot, steamy bowl
7 of porridge and then rush off? Where did they go? Maybe
8 somebody kidnapped them!

9   I just had to go in and check things out. Look for a clue
10 or something. They couldn't have just disappeared into thin
11 air, after all! I was going in to investigate. That's it. I wasn't
12 going to eat any porridge. I wasn't! It's just that I was awfully
13 hungry, and it smelled awfully good, and it was just sitting
14 there getting cold! I was going to take a little taste and be
15 done. Maybe even check to see if the porridge held a clue or
16 something.

17   But the first bowl was way too hot! It burned my tongue!
18 The second bowl was really cold! By the time I got to the third
19 bowl, which just happened to be perfect, I gobbled it all up! I
20 know I shouldn't have! But I couldn't resist! It was so good!
21 I'm really not a thief, I promise!

22   It doesn't matter, though, because I think they've
23 disappeared forever! Maybe they're not ever coming back.
24 *(Yawns.)* That porridge sure did make me sleepy! And all that
25 walking ...

26   I think I'll go take a tiny nap! I'll finish looking for clues
27 when I wake up.

I'm-Not-A-Blonde Gretel

1   Boys are so dumb! I told my brother we were going the
2 wrong way but would he listen? Noooo ... of course not! He
3 thinks he's so smart! He wouldn't even admit that we passed
4 the same tree at least three times!

5   I may be blonde, but even I could tell we were going in
6 circles! Of course he wouldn't stop and ask someone for
7 directions. Not a chance. He puffed up like a peacock and
8 said he had it all under control. I knew I never should've
9 followed him. I'm pretty sure he couldn't find his way out of a
10 paper bag, much less a huge overgrown forest.

11   And the whole bread crumb thing? Duh! Why didn't he
12 just feed the stinking animals right out of his hand? Was he
13 really stupid enough to think that would work? Maybe if he'd
14 been paying more attention to Mom and Dad instead of the
15 dumb breadcrumbs, we wouldn't have gotten lost in the first
16 place!

17   Our parents have to be frantic with worry by now! Daddy's
18 a hunter. He knows what kind of wild animals live in the
19 forest! He'll never sleep tonight knowing we're lost out here! I
20 can tell you this, when we do get found, Hansel is going to get
21 in so much trouble!

22   Especially when Mom finds out he talked to a stranger!
23 There we were, walking along, when we saw this house made
24 of candy. A house made of candy! Hello?! Red flag! I grabbed
25 Hansel and was ready to run, and he's waving at the lady! He
26 begged me to go in. "Look! She's inviting us in. I told you
27 things would work out OK! I am *so* hungry! Maybe she'll have
28 us for dinner!" he said. I swear for half a second I was ready
29 to let him go — alone! But even though he may be stupid,

1   he's still my brother! I just couldn't leave him that way!

2   Look at us now! Stuck in a pot! I guess there's one good

3   thing: We don't have to worry about being lost any more now,

4   do we?

Sleeping Like A Log
(and Loving It!) Beauty

1   I was having the most wonderful dream. Riding upon a
2   silver cloud, dipping down to drag my hand across a sky blue
3   river. Then I was standing in a meadow, surrounded by
4   flowers in every color of the rainbow. It was the most peaceful
5   feeling I've ever had. Every muscle in my body was relaxed. I
6   could feel myself falling deeper and deeper into sleep. It was
7   the most wonderful sensation!

8   Then, all of a sudden I was jerked awake! Pulled out of
9   my dreams like a car on a tow truck. Now my muscles are all
10 sore and stiff and I can barely move! I feel like I've barely slept
11 a moment, but in some ways it feels like ages!

12   Anyway, there I was, not bothering a soul, taking the nap
13 of a century, when that dude over there thinks he needs to
14 save me! Slay a dragon. Defeat a witch. Wake up a princess.
15 *Whatever*! Who said I wanted saving? Who said I *wanted* to
16 wake up?

17   I was all snuggly and warm, cozy as a bedbug! Doesn't he
18 know how hard it is to get into a deep sleep like that? It's
19 practically impossible!

20   But could he just leave me there all peaceful and dreamy?
21 No, of course not! He had to flex those muscles and show off!
22 Act like a hero. Like "Ooooh, the big bad prince can wake up
23 a princess." Big deal! Doesn't he have anything better to do
24 than go around messing up people's lives?

25   I swear that stinking prince has made me feel quite
26 grumpy! Where's my pillow? I think I'm in need of a nice long
27 nap!

18

Desperate Housewife:
Mrs. Claus

1   My husband works day and night! He never has any time
2   for me! All he does is work, work, work. He's a workaholic,
3   and I'm just sick of it! He's either hanging out in the stables
4   or checking out toys at the shop! And this is supposed to be
5   our slow season! What am I going to do when Christmas rolls
6   around? It's no wonder I've put on a few pounds! All I do is
7   eat! I'm bored to death.

8   Sure, I do the cleaning and the cooking. I even check the
9   mail! But do you know how depressing that is? A million
10 letters a day for my husband and not one single letter for me!
11 Not one! It's as if I don't even *exist*! Not even a bill in my
12 name! My own mother doesn't even write me!

13   "Get a hobby," he says. *Get a hobby*?! Doing what?
14 There's nothing to do in this snow-covered place. Nowhere to
15 go. He wouldn't dream of letting me take the sleigh, now
16 would he? Says it's got too much *power* for me to handle. I
17 think it's just his way of keeping the reins on me. He knows
18 if I had a chance to get out of here, I might never come back.

19   He gets to see the world every year. Me? I get nothing.
20 Same buildings, same snow, day in and day out. Well, I'm
21 tired of living this way. I deserve a vacation, and it's high time
22 I got one. If my dear old hubby knows what's good for him,
23 he'll hitch up that doggone sleigh and take me some place
24 warm and sunny! With *no snow*!

25   Yessiree! This Christmas we're going to Hawaii, whether
26 he likes it or not!

The Princess and the Pea-Brained Queen

1   Ooooh! I don't think I slept a wink last night! I tossed and
2   turned. But no matter how I tried, I could not get that
3   wretched noise out of my ears! At first I thought the castle
4   was under attack. I prayed that whatever howling creatures
5   had broken in wouldn't find me huddled beneath my mound
6   of covers.

7   Eventually I crept from my bed and found the real culprit:
8   The Queen. She snores louder than a herd of snorting pigs! I
9   couldn't believe so much noise could come from one person.
10   I tried to nudge her a little, but that only made it worse. It's
11   no wonder the King sleeps in a different wing.

12   Here I am supposed to be meeting my future husband
13   and look at me! I look like a nursemaid instead of a princess!
14   Can you see the bags under my eyes? I look older than his
15   mother, the Snore Queen, for heaven's sake!

16   I had to make up some ridiculous story about why I
17   couldn't sleep. I couldn't very well tell the truth, could I? She
18   could be my future mother-in-law for heaven's sake! Now
19   she's saying something about finding a pea under my
20   mattress and making a big deal about how lumpy it must've
21   been and no wonder I couldn't sleep ... is she kidding me? A
22   pea? Does she really think anyone's buying that? I could sleep
23   on a pile of rocks, I'm so tired!

24   There's really only one solution: More pillows. The fluffy,
25   feathery kind. I can stuff them around my head to muffle the
26   noise ...

27   ... Or I could just tiptoe in there with one of them and ...

28   Oh, I wouldn't really do it ... I swear ... but if I don't get
29   some sleep tonight, somebody's head is going to roll!

Thumbelina: Small But Sassy

1 When, oh when, am I ever going to get bigger? I'm tired of
2 being so awfully tiny! Do you know how many times I've
3 almost been stepped on, squashed like a bug? I'm always
4 watching for a shadow to fall over my head, knowing I have to
5 run or be stuck like a wad of gum to someone's shoe!

6 Everyone says things like how awesome it would be to be
7 tiny like me. "What an adventure!" they say. An *adventure*?
8 Are they crazy? It's more like *survival*!

9 I hardly ever leave the house anymore. It's way too
10 dangerous. I could drown in a foot-sized puddle, for heaven's
11 sake. Of course being inside is no picnic either. Yesterday, I
12 was trapped down in the garbage disposal for half the day. *Do*
13 *you know what would have happened if someone turned it*
14 *on*?! Mince-meat Thumbelina, that's what! Does that sound
15 like an adventure to you? Maybe if you like living a death
16 sentence!

17 After the ordeal with the disposal, you'd think I'd deserve
18 a break. But no! The stupid hairball they call a cat decided he
19 wanted to play — with me! Well, I'm no cat toy, I can tell you
20 that! I had to hide out in an empty mouse hole until that dumb
21 feline fell asleep. It made me miss my dinner! And I can barely
22 afford to do that. I only weigh a few ounces.

23 One day, when I get bigger, I'm going to teach that cat a
24 lesson!

The Forgetful Fairy Godmother

1   Oh, my, my, my! I'm all in a tizzy, I tell you! I've finally been
2 given a job — a real live "make a wish" job — and I can't find
3 my wand! That's been happening a lot lately. I found my hot
4 rollers in the fridge the other day. And my breakfast bagels
5 underneath the bathroom sink. I think all this spell-making has
6 re-wired my brain! I can't seem to do anything right! Yesterday, I
7 turned my cat into a frog, and I can't remember the spell to turn
8 her back. Have you ever seen a frog meow? It's quite disturbing,
9 let me tell you.
10   But what's a fairy godmother to do without a wand? I can't
11 whip up a fancy hairdo or beautiful gown with these crooked old
12 hands! Besides, I've never sewn a day in my life! And I certainly
13 can't pack Cinderella to the ball on my back!
14   Ooooh! What to do, what to do? I tell you the truth; I need my
15 own fairy godmother to help me. Oh, poor Cinderella! She's going
16 to be so disappointed having to wear those dirty old rags to the
17 ball! The Prince won't even notice her! Maybe she won't even go!
18 Oh, dear! Then they'll never meet! They'll never fall in love! And
19 they won't live happily ever after! She'll be stuck in this wretched
20 house with these wretched people, and it will all be my fault! Oh,
21 that just won't do!
22   *(As if calling for a dog)* Here little wand, here little wand! Oh, if
23 only I'd turned my cat into a dog instead! Then she could fetch it
24 for me. Why do I have to be so scatterbrained? It's like someone
25 put a curse on me.
26   It's just no use! I'm never going to find it. I'll probably be
27 demoted to tooth fairy now. I want to turn pumpkins into coaches,
28 not collect a bunch of dirty rotten teeth! I've got to find that wand
29 and find it fast! Maybe I should check the freezer … *(Rushes off.)*

Scissor-Happy Rapunzel

My hair is ruining my life. I'm just plain sick of it! I'd cut off every inch if I could! I would! Only I got stuck up in this tower with nary a pair of scissors or even a plain old butter knife! If I don't get it cut soon, I'm going to gnaw it off with my teeth!

For years and years my hair has grown — down my back, to the floor! Nobody has hair to the floor! It's quite ridiculous! I feel more like a hairy beast than a princess. I think it's part of my punishment — as if being locked up in this stupid tower isn't bad enough.

My hair is so long and so thick, it takes me all day to wash and dry it! By the time I'm done, it's time to start all over again! I used to hang it out the window on sunny days, just so it would dry faster, but not any more!

Do you know what happened to me? Some fool boy tried to climb up my hair! My *hair*! Like it was a rope! I would not make that up! I had to twist and shake and jerk my tresses until he fell off! Fell flat on his back in the bushes! Which is exactly what he deserved!

Can you imagine? Climbing up someone's hair? Who would do such a thing? It gave me quite a headache!

The Beastly Beauty

1   I've never had a feeling like this before. Never. Not in my
2 whole life. I'm in love. Love!
3   *(Looks to the left and gestures.)* With him? You're kidding
4 right? Have you *seen* him? All that hair? Ewwww ...
5 constantly have to pick hairs off my clothes. I've even had
6 them in my mouth at times! It's disgusting.
7   Of course it's not *him*. It's the *place* I'm in love with. I'd
8 do anything to live here. I've never been in a palace like this
9 before. It's gorgeous. The chandeliers, the tapestries, the
10 statues and fountains ... living here is like living in a dream.
11 It's practically as big as a city. I bet it even has its own zip
12 code!
13   There are so many rooms. My favorite is the library. All
14 those books — and all for me! The beast could care less
15 about reading. Probably doesn't even know *how* to read. But
16 I could stay in there for hours. In fact, most days I do. That's
17 another great thing about this place: I don't have to do
18 anything. There are tons of servants, and they do *everything!*
19 Back home I had to do all the chores: cleaning, cooking, doing
20 the wash. Why would I ever want to go back to that?
21   Sure, I miss my family. Especially my father. But one day
22 he'll be able to come visit. As soon as I convince the beast to
23 let him. I've seen his gray eyes staring at me during dinner. I
24 think he's falling in love. It's just a matter of time before I
25 have him wrapped around my finger. Then I'll be able to do
26 whatever I want. He thinks I'm his "prisoner." What a joke.
27 In a few more weeks, he'll be doing everything I say. Maybe
28 I'll even be able to get him to cut that hideous hair!

Star-Struck Little Bo Peep

1 I know everyone thinks I lost the sheep because I'm
2 blonde. They do. They make stupid blonde jokes all the time.
3 But I don't care because I know the truth. One, I'm not really
4 blonde. I mean, come on, do you really think this kind of
5 golden color doesn't come out of a box? Get real. And two, I
6 didn't lose those stupid smelly sheep. How could I possibly
7 lose a whole flock of sheep?

8 I took them somewhere far away so I could be rid of them.
9 Do you have any idea how boring it is sitting in a field,
10 watching sheep all day? Picture yourself watching your
11 toenails grow. Yup. It's *that* exciting.

12 And smelly. They don't just stand there, you know. They
13 make all these little "piles." All day long. Eat, sleep, "baa"
14 like crazy, and go to the bathroom. It's a real joy being a part
15 of *that* day in and day out. Especially when the sun is hot and
16 that breeze just won't stop blowing in your face. Most people
17 wouldn't last a day, much less all these years I've been stuck
18 doing it.

19 If there'd *been* a cliff nearby, I just *might* have walked
20 them off it! But I didn't. I swear. I'm not *that* mean. I just
21 needed to get rid of them so I could pursue my *real* career:
22 Singing. See, I've been practicing since I was really little.
23 Singing the sheep to sleep, singing the sheep awake. It's the
24 only way I've been able to stand it. So make all the blonde
25 jokes you want. Now that I'm free and clear of those stupid
26 sheep, I'm off to be a star!

The Just-As-Pretty Stepsister

1   I don't see why everyone thinks she's *so* pretty. You just
2   have to look a little harder to see that her nose is actually
3   somewhat off-center. And her eyes are not all that blue. Her
4   hair has split ends, and she hides her acne with tons of
5   makeup. So, OK, from a *distance*, she may seem like a real
6   beauty. But up close, she's practically a dog.

7   Maybe if I wore all that makeup, they'd think I was pretty,
8   too. But do I have a chance? Of course not. The minute the
9   doorbell rings, there she is. By the time I get there, the Avon
10 lady is long gone. Cinderella thinks I don't know what she's
11 up to, but I do. She cherishes the fact that everyone calls my
12 sister and me the *ugly stepsisters*. But how can we have a
13 chance when she's hogging the Avon lady? Who knows what
14 a makeover could do for me?

15 Oh, and she's keeping us fat on purpose! She is. I've
16 begged for her to bring me salad for lunch, but she never
17 does. "I'm sorry. I forgot," she'll say. "I could run to town and
18 get some lettuce if you really want me to." Do you *know* how
19 long that would take? It would be dinnertime when she got
20 back, and I'd be starving to death! She fixes totally fattening
21 meals. Mashed potatoes and gravy. All kinds of casseroles.

22 Everything's cooked in butter. She bakes cookies, pies,
23 and cakes every day. She may be dead ugly, but man can she
24 cook! It's completely impossible to resist her crumb cakes.
25 And her cheesecake is to die for. It's no wonder my sister,
26 mother, and I are all fat as cows. It's like we live in a bakery!
27 Who can stay skinny in this house? Well, *she* can. I haven't
28 figured that one out yet. I think maybe she's allergic to sugar
29 or something 'cause you *never* see her stuffing her face with

1   one of her pastries. Never. It's like she's immune to their
2   heavenly smell.
3   I know! It's that crooked nose of hers! It doesn't smell
4   things quite right! All I know is, we're like her prisoners! If she
5   keeps us fat and ugly, no one will ever want *us*!

Boy-Crazy Little Miss Muffet

1   Afraid of a little spider like that? You've got to be kidding
2 me. It was all an act. A big, *huge* act to get those boys over
3 there to notice me. It worked, too. I let out a little squeal and
4 they practically tripped over themselves getting here.

5   "I'll get it," one said. "No! Let me!" another one said. "I'm
6 the oldest. I'll get it!" the tall one said. It was actually quite
7 comical. They stood there fighting over who was going to
8 squash it, yet nobody would *actually* do it. Honestly, I think
9 they were all afraid. I noticed that every time the spider
10 moved toward them, they all jumped back. Not exactly
11 dragon-slaying material, I'd have to say.

12   Still, I tried to play the fair maiden. I kept squealing and
13 jumping up and down, trying to act quite faint. All the while
14 they stood there, shoes in hand, arguing about who would do
15 it. The whole act was getting quite tiring.

16   I tried nudging them along; "Kill it! Oh, *please* kill it!" I
17 screeched while I fanned my face and tried to look like I was
18 about to faint. I thought a little direction might help them out
19 since they seemed clueless as to what to do. They'd raise a
20 shoe and get real close. That poor petrified spider would jump
21 a little and those boys would just about pee their pants. I'd
22 never seen such a bunch of scaredy cats. A girl can only take
23 so much! I grabbed a shoe, and whack ... no more itsy bitsy
24 spider!

Stamp-Collecting
Old Mother Hubbard

1   Look at this! *(Holds out a piece of paper.)* Are they for real?
2 "Condemned"? They can't condemn my home! Where am I gonna
3 put all these kids? How am I supposed to raise all these younguns
4 without a home?
5   I know this shoe ain't much, but it's ours. And it's all we got.
6 Their daddy left us high and dry a long time ago. I've been struggling
7 ever since. I don't hardly have any food in my cupboards, and their
8 clothes are all threadbare.
9   Course, if the government would give me a little more money
10 every month, I wouldn't be doing so bad. How do they expect me to
11 feed all these mouths on what they give me? It's a crime how little I
12 get. Don't they care about us starving? If it wasn't for our garden out
13 back, we'd never make it.
14   And look at this! A letter telling me to get a job. Get a job!
15 Where's a woman with twenty kids going to work? All my pay would
16 go to day care. Do they even think about that? No. The government
17 don't care about me and my kids.
18   They say I've got until Friday to get my kids out of this shoe and
19 into another home. Where's that supposed to be? It's like those
20 government officials are living in a fairy tale, they are. Thinking I got
21 somewhere to go. You see anyone opening their doors to me? Heck
22 no. Most times people shut and lock their doors when they see my
23 kids and me coming.
24   It's all because I'm a woman. That's what it is. If I was a man,
25 they wouldn't be treating me this way. Giving me these things called
26 food stamps that won't even let me get my ciggies! It's atrocious the
27 way they treat me. Like I'm a criminal or something just 'cause I got
28 so many kids! Well, can I help it that I love the little buggers so
29 much? I'm so distraught I just don't know what to do!

Card-Carrying Pocahontas

1   Now, you can't tell anybody you saw this! If you do, I'll be
2 ruined. Could you just see their faces? The nature-loving
3 Indian girl — a card-carrying member of the NRA! But I can't
4 help it. I love the thrill of the hunt. I've been hunting since I
5 was a little girl. Except back then we only had bows and
6 arrows. It was hard to peg a really good kill. Although I have
7 to say, I was quite good.

8   Daddy would never let me bring home the animals,
9 though. Said it wouldn't look right that his daughter could
10 outhunt the men in the tribe. He made me keep it our little
11 secret. I didn't mind because keeping it a secret made it seem
12 dangerous, and I love danger!

13   Anyway, I was fine using my bow and arrow and keeping
14 things on the sly. But then these explorers came, and you
15 should've seen what they had. Guns! I couldn't believe it! I
16 made friends with those guys real quick. It didn't take long for
17 them to trust me. One day I traded some corn for a gun. I
18 could tell they didn't want to trade for it, but in the end, they
19 did. I guess they thought since I was just a girl it didn't really
20 matter. Probably figured I'd never even learn how to shoot it!

21   Well, were they ever wrong! I can shoot a corncob off a
22 tree stump at fifty paces. There's this one guy, John Smith,
23 who thinks he's really good. I'd love to show him a thing or
24 two about shooting, but I know I can't. He thinks I'm all
25 earthy — flowers and butterflies, you know? He'd die if he
26 knew the truth. Probably call me a "savage" like he did that
27 day I first met him. I really don't have a choice. I have to stay
28 friendly if I want to be able to trade for more gunpowder.

Secret Agent
Little Red Riding Hood

1   All that work — for nothing! All those practices — down
2 the drain! Why did I even bother getting my black belt? What
3 good is it ever going to do me? I finally get the chance to use
4 it *(Does a few karate chops in the air)* and here comes the big,
5 bad woodsman to save the day. Couldn't he see that I had it
6 all under control? I was going to pound on that wolf's head, I
7 tell you. Had it all planned out. I'd even gotten in a kick or two
8 before the woodsman ruined everything.

9   I'd been following that wolf for weeks trying to pin
10 something on him. I knew without a doubt that he was bad to
11 the core. I just didn't have any proof. The little red riding hood
12 thing was brilliant. He'd never suspect a helpless young girl on
13 her way to see her grandma. Ha! I laugh at the thought of me
14 being helpless! I'm at the top of my karate class!

15   The basket of goodies was just too much to resist. That
16 stupid wolf trailed me all the way up the mountain. Ducking
17 behind trees. Crouching down beside bushes. He wasn't very
18 clever at hiding, I can tell you that. You would've thought he
19 could make his way through the jungle without sounding like
20 a mad elephant on the loose!

21   I didn't think he was ever going to take the lead and beat
22 me there. I had to stop and tie my shoes twice just to give
23 him a head start. Even then, I could hear the pitiful thing
24 puffing like crazy. I was afraid I might have to give him mouth-
25 to-mouth resuscitation and save his life instead of capturing
26 him!

27   But it was all going according to plan. I could taste my
28 success. The lady I hired to play my grandma played her part
29 excellently. By the time I got there, she'd let the wolf tie her

1   up and stuff her in the closet, just like I'd told her to.

2   But then it all went down the drain. All that work. All that

3   planning. For nothing. The woodsman stole the show. I ended

4   up looking like a scared little girl and the woodsman came out

5   the hero. Guess the one good thing is I kept my cover. Secret

6   Agent Little Red Riding Hood, at your service.

Dust-Dealin' Tinkie

1　　Have you ever felt used? That somebody always wants
2　something from you? That if you didn't have that *one* thing
3　they want, they wouldn't even look your way? Well, that's how
4　I feel. Only time anyone ever calls me is when they want
5　something. Otherwise, I never hear from them. But get in a
6　pickle and need some help ...

7　　"Tink. Tink. Can I have some dust?"

8　　"Just a little, OK? I'll make it last. I promise."

9　　"Just this last time. I swear, Tink. Cross my heart and
10　hope to die."

11　　"I'll give it up next week, Tink. I promise."

12　　Bull! It's like they're addicted to the stuff! Makes me feel
13　like a dealer. Seems like nowadays everyone wants a chance
14　to fly. What's wrong with their feet, that's what I'd like to
15　know! Don't they know I'm not made of pixie dust? And even
16　if I was, why should I give it to them? It's not my job to supply
17　the world with dust!

18　　Besides, what's anybody ever done for me? I don't owe
19　them anything. The only one that's ever loved me for me is
20　sweet Peter. He's my best friend in the whole world. He's in
21　there right now trying to get his shadow back. Then he and I
22　are going to fly back to Never-Never Land.

23　　*(Taps foot.)* This is taking longer than I thought. How long
24　does it take to grab a shadow, anyway?

Dog-Lovin' Mary

1   This stupid lamb is getting on my last nerve! He follows
2 me absolutely everywhere I go. You know what he did
3 yesterday? Followed me into the bathroom! And after that he
4 followed me to school. Do you know how much trouble I got
5 in? I was the laughingstock for the whole day! They sang this
6 ridiculous rhyme about me having a lamb. How did they even
7 come up with it that fast? It's like they pulled it out of thin
8 air!
9   But could you blame them? I mean, come on! Who has a
10 lamb for a pet, anyway? Especially a clingy, obsessive-
11 compulsive lamb that follows you absolutely everywhere you
12 go? What were my parents thinking? Was it some kind of
13 joke? We live in an apartment, not on a farm!
14   I begged them for a dog. A cute, fluffy dog that I could
15 teach how to fetch and shake hands. A *small* animal that
16 would sleep in my bed and sit on my lap. This thing takes up
17 the whole bed and chews on my covers. And all that wool
18 makes me sweat like a pig! It's like sleeping with a heater —
19 in the middle of summer!
20   Now I'm not saying he's not cute. I mean, look at those
21 big brown eyes. And his pink nose is pretty sweet, too. But
22 he's a lamb! He belongs in a field, not following me around. I
23 just wanted a dog. Plain and simple. What was hard about
24 that? I'm never going to live this down. I can tell that people
25 will be talking about me for years and years to come.

Not-So-Forgetful Anastasia

"I don't know." "I can't remember." "I don't even know who I am." Pretty good, huh? I've been serving up those lame lines since I was a little girl. Everyone thinks the trauma of what happened affected my brain somehow. They think that I have amnesia and can't remember anything that happened that day. They also think I'm missing. But I'm not. I know exactly *who* and *where* I am.

In fact, I remember every single gory detail. It was tragic. The worst thing I'd ever seen in my life. There are plenty of days I wish I didn't remember a single thing. That I really *could* have amnesia and never see those things in my mind again.

How can they seriously think I could block all of that out? Wishful thinking, I'm sure. Especially on my Grandmamma's part. She wants the whole world to think she's the doting, distraught grandmother who lost her granddaughter all those years ago.

Lost, my foot! She let go of me on purpose. My little legs weren't able to keep up with hers. She kept saying, "Run faster, Anastasia." What did she think I was doing? I remember thinking that if I ran any faster, I'd probably start flying. I begged her to slow down, but she just kept pulling me after her.

The train was right in front of us, already starting to pull away from the station. The wheels were churning faster and faster. I knew there was no way we were going to make it. I was right. *We* didn't. But Grandmamma did. She was getting out of there no matter what. Even if it meant letting go of my hand and leaving me at the station. Alone.

1   So why would I want to tell anyone who I really am? What
2 do you think they'd do first? Ship me off to my grandmamma,
3 of course. Why would I want to live with her? I'd rather be here
4 at this orphanage living with six other girls in my room than
5 living in the palace with her! Does she really think I could ever
6 forgive her?

Crown-Breaking Jill

1   *(In a very whiny voice)* "Will you come with me?" "I can't
2 do it myself." "The pail is way too heavy."

3   *(In normal voice)* I swear that boy was getting on my last
4 nerve! He can't do anything by himself. I fetch pails of water
5 all the time, and do I ask him for help? No, of course not! He'd
6 be more of a hindrance than a help anyway. Even when I have
7 to help him, I'm the one who ends up carrying the pail most
8 of the way home.

9   And that crown! Don't even get me started on that! Does
10 he think he's a king or something? He never takes that stupid
11 thing off. He told me it gives him special powers. Well, it
12 certainly isn't strength, I can tell you that! The only power
13 he's got is *dork* power!

14   Even though he is the most annoying boy, I still feel bad
15 about what happened. He's been crying ever since. I told him
16 I'd try to fix his stupid crown, but he won't even let me see it.
17 Says it's all my fault, even though I told him it was an
18 *accident* — which it *wasn't*.

19   I just didn't know that he'd trip so hard. I only stuck my
20 foot out a little. Any normal kid could've righted himself right
21 away — but not Jack. Oh, no! He took a tumble all the way
22 down that hill. Worst part was, so did I! That stupid boy
23 grabbed me when he started to fall! We must've looked like a
24 snowball gathering speed. I swear my new motto is: If you
25 want something done, you should do it yourself!

National Pop Star: Rejected and in Denial

1   *(Walks in sobbing.)* I just ... don't ... get it ... everyone says
2   I sing like an ... angel. I've been in the church choir since I
3   was only five years old. And one time when I was in fifth
4   grade, I sang the National Anthem over the loudspeaker for
5   the whole school to hear. It was only scratchy because of the
6   P.A. system. Even the teachers said they knew I must've sung
7   better in person!

8   *(Distraught)* Why would Steven Scowl say such mean
9   things? Doesn't he know a good singer when he hears one?
10 Isn't that, like, his job or something? To find talent? He didn't
11 even give me a chance! Barely even looked at me!

12   If he had, he would've seen what a great dancer I am, too
13 *(Makes funky/jerky dance movement.)* But no! He was too busy
14 doodling on his paper ... and laughing! At me! Why would he
15 laugh at me? Singing isn't funny.

16   Why didn't he give me a chance? I can sing. I can. Listen:
17 *(Sings badly.)* Mary had a Little Lamb, Little Lamb. *(Stops
18 singing.)* See? A voice like an angel.

19   *(Pauses, then has an "Aha!" moment.)* That's it! I'm just too
20 good for this show! No one would be able to compete with me.
21 That's what Steven meant when he said I had a voice like
22 nobody else's! It's too good! Too perfect! Everyone else would
23 sound horrible compared to me, and the show would be
24 ruined!

25   Oh, Steven! You're brilliant! I love you!

Kitten with a Stolen Mitten

1 *(Sniffs as if crying.)* **My** momma's gonna kill me. She told
2 me not to take them off.

3 "Not once," she said.

4 "Not even if you have an itch," she said.

5 And I didn't. Not once. Have an itch, that is. Although my
6 nose did get a tickle, but after a couple of twitches, it was OK.
7 So I didn't take my mitten off for something silly like a little
8 itch! I didn't! It was way more important than that!

9 *(Whispers.)* **See,** I found this berry bush — and it still had
10 berries! And so I started eating some. Only I kept getting fuzz
11 in my mouth. And fuzzy berries aren't very good. In fact,
12 they're really quite icky! So I *had* to take my mitten off! There
13 was no other way.

14 I just took *one* mitten off! I was only going to eat a few
15 berries and then put it back on. But now it's gone!
16 Disappeared into thin air. I've looked everywhere, and I can't
17 find my stupid mitten!

18 Maybe a raccoon, or a rat, or even a lion has run off with
19 it. Snatched it from right under my nose. I know I'll never see
20 that fuzzy blue thing again! Momma's gonna be real mad.
21 She'll never believe it was stolen and not lost! I'm the victim,
22 not the culprit! Anybody can see that!

23 *(Pause)* **Hey,** maybe if I hold one paw behind my back,
24 she'll never notice!

Living Large Barbie

1   I've got the greatest life! I do! I have more clothes than
2   anyone I know! All kinds, too! Fancy clothes, sports clothes,
3   casual clothes! Every kind a girl could want!

4   My sisters, Kelly and Stacey, are always trying to fit in
5   them, but of course they can't! I mean, look at this body! It's
6   absolutely perfect. Not a single flaw. It's like I came from a
7   mold, for heaven's sake! My clothes fit me like a glove, as if
8   they were made especially for me and no one else.

9   I've got tons of shoes, too! In every color and style! Oh,
10   sometimes I can't find the matches, but that's OK because I
11   have so many to choose from! And they fit like a glove. Slip
12   a pair on and I'm ready to party! I even have roller blades and
13   cowboy boots. I am so lucky!

14   But shoes and clothes are nothing compared to the other
15   things I have! Would you believe I own a pink convertible, a
16   blue van, a camper, a bus, a boat, a horse, and a plane? A
17   plane! Can you believe that? How many girls my age have a
18   boat *and* a plane?

19   I live in a cool house, too. With an elevator and everything.
20   Sometimes it feels a little open and drafty, but I wouldn't
21   move for the world! Even my furniture is super-cool. Almost
22   everything is pink — my absolute favorite color!

23   Can you believe that I used to live in a box? I could barely
24   breathe it was so claustrophobic. But look at me now! I'm
25   living the life of a star!

The Little Con Girl

1   People are so gullible. Smudge on a little dirt, put a few rips
2 in the old clothes, and voila! Little poor girl in need of some
3 money. I've been working this corner for six months and nobody's
4 the wiser. I've almost saved up enough money to buy a car! And
5 I'm only fourteen. If I keep at it, I'll probably be able to buy a house
6 before I even graduate from high school.

7   It's so easy. I go to these restaurants — the real fancy kinds
8 with cloth napkins and candles on the tables. The ones with the
9 free stuff. Mints. Toothpicks. And best of all, matches! I grab a
10 couple of handfuls, and I've got free merchandise to peddle on the
11 corner! Just last week someone gave me a twenty — for a pack
12 of matches!

13   I don't think the woman even smoked. Hardly anyone does
14 anymore. But that doesn't matter, because they still give me
15 money. Most of the time they don't even take the matches. "You
16 keep them, honey," they'll say, and then they'll press a five dollar
17 bill into my hand. A fiver for a pack of matches!

18   Why would anyone work when they can do something as easy
19 as this? Oh, I know what you're thinking — that I'm stealing from
20 those poor people. But I'm not. Not if you think about it. People
21 pay to go to the movies, right? And that money goes to actors and
22 actresses, right? Well, that's what I am! An actress playing the
23 part of a poor little match girl. Can I help it that I'm so good
24 everyone actually believes me? And if I *am* that good that I can
25 really convince people, than *shouldn't* I get paid? Heck, I'm
26 starting to think I should win an Oscar!

27   Oh! I gotta go! Here comes somebody.

28   *(Looks pitiful, with head down and cocked to the side.)* **"Matches.**
29 **Matches for sale."**

Angela the
Disgruntled Babysitter

1   These babies are getting on my nerves! They're
2 disgusting! Do you know where they go to the bathroom? In
3 their pants! Anytime, anywhere! And it doesn't even bother
4 them. In fact, I think they like it. One time, they used their
5 poopie to paint pictures on the walls. You should've seen my
6 Aunt Debby's face!

7   But did those smelly babies get in trouble? Of course not!
8 "Angela! Why weren't you watching them! Look at this mess!
9 Well, you're going to clean it up, young lady!" she said and
10 then she gave me some 'splies *(Supplies)* and left the room.

11   I used three whole paper towel rolls to clean up that wall!
12 And I didn't even get to watch my favorite TV show. But did
13 those babies care? No, they just crawled off to get into more
14 trouble! Or make some kind of mess that I'll have to clean up.

15   It's just not fair! All the time I'm stuck watching them like
16 they was my kids or something! Hello, peoples! I'm only four
17 years old. I am not qualdified *(Qualified)* to be no babysitter.
18 Besides, babysitters get paid, and no one ever gives me no
19 money! Not even Mommy, and she's got this really 'portant
20 *(Important)* job where she talks on her cellar *(Cellular)* phone
21 all the time.

22   *(Pause)* Hey! I want a job like that! Gabbing on the phone
23 and not being with stupid babies who drool and go poopie in
24 their pants.

25   Look! Aunt Debby left her phone right here in her purse!
26 All I gots to do is pick it up and push some buttons and yell
27 at the people on the other end and then I can be 'portant, too!
28 *(Pantomimes picking up phone and pushing buttons.)* **So long,**
29 **stupid babies!**

Runaway Bride: Mrs. Frankenstein

1   You've got to hide me! I don't have anywhere else to go.
2   *(Acts like he's listening to something Off-stage.)* Do you hear that?
3   It's him! I've only just met him, and I'd recognize that earth-
4   shaking stomp anywhere. He's coming after me!

5   *(Paces)* Why did I ever agree to an arranged marriage? I
6   should've known something was wrong. "It'll add to the
7   romance," that stupid scientist said when he came up with
8   the idea. "Just think how surprised you'll be when Frankie
9   lifts your veil. It'll be a moment to remember."

10   Well, he was right about that! I'll never forget that moment
11   for the rest of my life. I wasn't surprised — I was terrified! The
12   man had *bolts* sticking out of his neck, for heaven's sake! Why
13   would I ever marry such a monster?

14   Of course now I am married to him! He didn't lift the veil
15   until the very end ... which was weird, now that I think about
16   it — don't they usually do that at the beginning? Anyhow,
17   we'd already said the whole "I do" thing. But I *don't*! I really,
18   really don't! I can't be married to such a hideous man!

19   To think I almost kissed him! Thank goodness I opened
20   my eyes right as his head was coming toward me! And what
21   a head! It's practically *square*! And it's all scarred up. He's got
22   more stitches than a patchwork quilt! Like someone put that
23   hideous face together!

24   That's why you've got to hide me! Save me from a life with
25   that ... thing! I promise, as soon as the coast is clear, I'm
26   getting out of here and getting an annulment!

Funky Friday Forever

1   *(Holding hand to head, perplexed)* I don't know what I drank
2   last night but it must have been the fountain of youth! Either
3   I'm very, very drunk or something amazing has happened!
4   Look at me! All young and in shape. Everything firm and tight.
5   What could I possibly wear? Like a size two? This body is
6   incredible! Curved in all the *right* places! No wrinkles. No
7   sagging. No extra flab! It's a dream come true. I haven't had
8   a stomach this flat since ... oh, who am I kidding? I've *never*
9   had a stomach this flat!
10   The weird thing is I look exactly like my daughter! I always
11   thought we looked a lot alike, but this is eerie. I look like her
12   *twin*!
13   Oh, she's going to flip when she sees me! She'll be so
14   embarrassed to have her mom looking as young as she is.
15   Well, tough cookies, baby! I wouldn't give this body up for
16   anything! Mama's had a miracle body-lift, and she's keeping
17   it!
18   *(Pause)* Why am I in Annie's room? I must've really been
19   out of it if I came in here ... my room isn't even upstairs. And
20   if I'm in here ... where's Annie? Surely she didn't stay out all
21   night! I'd better go find ... *(Begins to rush out but suddenly*
22   *stops.)* Ooooh look at this cute little sweater! *(Pantomines*
23   *holding it up.)* Why, I bet I could fit in it! *(Pantomimes putting it*
24   *on.)* I can! Look at me. All hip and in fashion! I'll be the
25   coolest mom in town! Wait till Annie sees me! *(Rushes Off-*
26   *stage.)*

Mary Boppins

1   *(In a British accent, if possible)* **It's always the same. Parents**
2   wait until their wretched little darlings are tearing up the
3   house and then they call me. "Help us, Mary Boppins! We
4   can't control our kids any more!" Well, news flash! You never
5   *could* because you never *did*! Children don't just pop out of
6   control overnight! You grow them into these obnoxious
7   buggers!
8   No rules. No chores. No punishments. No bed times. No
9   schedules. It's utter chaos! You wouldn't believe the things
10   I've seen! Ice cream for breakfast. Rooms you need a shovel
11   to get through. Backtalk and hitting. A mum who got a black
12   eye — from a three-year-old!
13   These parents want me to pity them! But it's the children
14   I feel sorry for! You can't expect them to be good when they
15   don't know any better. It's like taking away the speed limit
16   and expecting drivers to go a safe speed!
17   I do the best I can, but I half-expect that everything goes
18   back to the way it was after I leave. Just as children don't go
19   bad overnight, parents don't learn to be better parents
20   overnight, either. But maybe I've taught them something
21   about *organization*.
22   Sometimes, though rarely, there are *too many rules.*
23   Children brought up as if they're in the military, for crying out
24   loud. Not allowed to be kids. That's the case where I'm at
25   now. The father runs a tight ship. He's so bloody busy belting
26   out orders and treating his children like soldiers that they
27   don't have any time to be children! They're not allowed to get
28   dirty or have any fun a'tall!
29   For once, it wasn't the parents who called for me. It was

1   the children! They're craving someone to pay attention to
2   them, and that's what I'm going to do. No rules! They've got
3   plenty of them! Just some good old fun. Maybe we'll make a
4   sidewalk drawing and jump right in it! Won't that be a hoot?
5   Now let's see what I've got in my carpetbag.

Mary the Matchmaker

1   I've got it all figured out. It's not like it was rocket science or
2   anything. There are four guys and three girls. Of course, Mr. and
3   Mrs. Powell already have each other, so that takes them out of the
4   running. Which leaves Skip, the scholar, and Billigan for Cinnamon
5   and me. It makes perfect sense that Cinnamon would get Skip.
6   She loves that powerful military type. And I would get the scholar
7   since we're both smart and sensible. I feel sorry that Billigan
8   doesn't have anyone, but he's just a kid. Too goofy to be anyone's
9   husband.
10   If we're going to be stuck on this island, it only makes sense
11   that we hook up with one another! Otherwise our whole species
12   could die out! We'll just sit here until we rot into non-existence!
13   Skip can perform the ceremonies and then we can all live happily
14   ever after.
15   It's a great plan! One that could really work ... if it wasn't for
16   Cinnamon. She's such a flirt! She's just not happy if *all* the men
17   aren't drooling all over her. Even Mr. Powell, and he's married!
18   How can I get the scholar to look my way with her around! It's
19   ridiculous that she even wears those get-ups! We're not in
20   Hollywood anymore. Heels and an evening gown are *not*
21   appropriate island wear!
22   She acts all innocent and dumb. Like she can't do anything
23   for herself. How hard is it to crack your own coconut! She'll pout
24   those perfect little lips until those men are falling all over
25   themselves to help her. It's sickening to watch.
26   What am I supposed to do? Let her have all of them? Well, I'm
27   not going down without a fight. Two can play her little game.
28   *(Pantomimes pulling down her blouse a little and pulling up her skit a*
29   *little to make it shorter.)* **Oh, Scholar! Could you help me with this?**

Indignant Patsy Pig

1 Moi? In love with a frog? You've got to be kidding. Why would
2 someone like me be in love with a scrawny little green thing like
3 him! Squeaky voice. Pointed webbed feet. Googly bug eyes and
4 that silly little collar! What could a beautiful specimen like myself
5 possibly find attractive about that?

6 How do rumors like these get started? I've only treated Hermit
7 with utmost respect and professionalism. Nothing to feed the
8 flames of such gossip! They all must be trying to cause a scandal
9 to get me fired! They're jealous of all the attention I get. But can
10 I help it if I'm so much better than them? Maybe if they had a little
11 talent they wouldn't stoop to such levels!

12 Who could believe such a thing anyway? Hermie and I — we're
13 like night and day. Peanut butter and jelly. Cheese and crackers.
14 Sweet and sour! I'm strong. He's weak. I'm loud. He's soft. I'm
15 big — *well, in comparison to him!* He's a pipsqueak!

16 Can't everyone see? We're complete opposites! If we got
17 together it'd be an abomination! We'd never get along. He'd pull
18 one way, I'd pull another. The fighting would be nonstop! So much
19 anger ... so much *passion!*

20 *(Very excited — her true feelings have burst out of her.)* I'd be the
21 Ginger to his Fred Astaire. The Lucy to his Ricky! The Eve to his
22 Adam. The moon to his stars! Oh, Hermie! Why can't you see
23 that we were made for each other! You complete me! We're two
24 halves that make a whole! Two peas in a pod! Two ships that
25 *shouldn't* pass in the night! Oh, Hermie! We were meant to be
26 together! Come back! I didn't mean it when I called you a
27 pipsqueak! You're absolutely adorable! You know that! Hermie! I
28 love you!

Wendy-Lou the Whiner

1   Why do I always get stuck watching the boys? Can't Mom
2 and Dad get a bona fide babysitter and give me a break? I'm
3 tired of wiping noses, cleaning up messes, and reading
4 endless bedtime stories. When do I get time for myself? To
5 soak in a bath, paint my nails, have a facial? Things a girl is
6 supposed to do!

7   This house is in testosterone overload. It's all about
8 burping and booger jokes! Do you have any idea how gross
9 brothers can be? Or what it's like being the only girl? We never
10 do anything I want to do. It's all roughhousing and bed
11 jumping and pillow fights! I'm about to lose my mind! That's
12 why I need to get out and spend some time with my friends!

13   I want to talk about makeup and fashion and all the latest
14 celebrities! Go out to the movies or shopping at the mall! *Girl*
15 things! Instead I'm always stuck listening to the boys babble
16 on about Indians and pirates and all sorts of nonsense.

17   *(Pause)* **Maybe I could sneak out … the boys have been**
18 asleep for hours. I could just slip out this window … the dog
19 won't bark if she knows it's me! And I'll be back long before
20 Mom and Dad get home. They never get home before
21 midnight, always out having fun. Well, I deserve to have a little
22 fun, too.

23   *(Pantomimes opening window and climbing through.)* **Girl's**
24 **Night Out, here I come!**

Pippi Longsock's Bad Hair Day

1   I straighten and I straighten and I straighten this dag-
2 blasted hair, and for what? The second I step outside, it's like
3 I got caught in an electrical storm! Instant frizzy!
4   I can't do a thing with it. Well, that's not completely true.
5 I *can* braid it. Do you know how utterly sick I am of *braids*?
6 They're fine for a six-year-old, but I'm almost sixteen! Here I
7 am about ready to drive, and I look like I'm too young for a
8 PG-thirteen movie.
9   But what choice do I have but to braid it? If I leave it
10 down, it looks like clown hair. Slap a rubber red nose on my
11 face and I'd be the life of the party.
12   I've tried conditioner, hair spray — I used a *whole can*
13 one time — frizz control. I've even tried gobs of *lard*! That's
14 kitchen grease for you city girls! The only thing that did was
15 make me afraid to go near an open flame!
16   It's like my hair is out to get me. Torture me for the rest
17 of my life. Worst part is, Prom is coming up, and I've actually
18 got a date. What the heck am I going to do about my hair? I
19 can't wear braids! But what choice do I have? A hat? How
20 about I just put a *bag* over my head?
21   I swear, one day I'm just going to *shave* it all off! Every
22 last frizzy strand ... hey ... that could actually work. One great
23 wig and no one would be the wiser! I'll have the best hairdo
24 at the Prom!

Mrs. Snack Man,
Former Fatkins Spokesperson

1   Look at me! Just look at me! I'm as tall as I am round!
2   It's absolutely ridiculous how fat I am! I've been watching my
3   diet for years now. Munching those tasteless dots with *zero*
4   carbs, and for what? Have I even lost a single pound? *No!* Even
5   my energy dots are carb-free, and I'm still gaining weight!

6   And a diet just isn't a diet without exercise, right? Well,
7   I've been running my butt off, night and day, and I've got more
8   junk in my trunk than a car packed for vacation! Who came
9   up with this idiotic stuff? My carb counter might as well say
10   *fat counter*! The only way my scale has been going is up!

11   I think this Fatkins thing is a load of bull. It sure hasn't
12   helped me! I don't even cheat ... well, not really. Sure I might
13   have a piece of fruit now and then ... but only because I get
14   so tired of eating all those dots! A person can't live on one
15   food group alone! And besides, I run around to get it, so
16   shouldn't that count for something?

17   Maybe it's time to try something else — like the cabbage
18   soup diet! Or the low-fat, no-taste diet! Maybe I could go
19   sugar-free. I hear Splenda tastes pretty good. If all else fails,
20   I could try the North Beach diet. But that sounds way too
21   trendy to me. I'm an old-fashioned kind of girl.

22   You know what? I say to heck with diets! There's nothing
23   wrong with me! I don't have to be a skinny toothpick girl! I can
24   be as round as I want. In fact, you can just call me "full-
25   figured!"

Princess Liona,
Divorce Court Defendant

1   *(As if talking on the phone)* **Hello? Mummy? It's me. Liona.**

2   **I need your help ... see, I've done something stupid ... what?**

3   **... No. I did not say anything about cupid ... I can't speak up.**

4   **He might hear me. ... You don't know his temper. Just listen**

5   **carefully.**

6   **See, I'm calling to tell you that I got married. Mummy,**

7   **stop screaming! You've got to listen to me! And stop yelling**

8   **at the servants, you are *not* organizing a reception! ... No,**

9   **that's not why I've called. ... I don't know why I did it — I**

10   **guess I was under a spell or something ... Stop crying ... I am**

11   **not trying to break your heart. If you'd just listen ...**

12   **I need you and Daddy to get me out of this fiasco ... yes,**

13   **I *know* marriage is *forever*, but you don't understand,**

14   **Mummy! I married an ogre! ... Of course I'm not talking about**

15   **the prince you sent to rescue me. He never showed up! I**

16   **swear I'm telling the truth! I married an ogre!**

17   **I am *not* exaggerating ... I know I used to make up**

18   **ridiculous stories ... No, I don't mean he's just messy ... Yes,**

19   **Mummy, I know how men are. Listen to me! He's not a man!**

20   **He's big and green and his breath smells like a thousand**

21   **rotten onions! In fact, every time he kisses me, it makes my**

22   **eyes water! I can't stay married to someone like that. I'm a**

23   **princess ...**

24   **Well, I was a princess. Now I look like him! You've got to**

25   **send Fairy Godmother to help me — change me back to**

26   **normal and get me out of this swamp. This place is**

27   **disgusting! ... No, don't send the prince! I would die if he saw**

28   **me this way!**

29   *(As if hearing something Off-stage)* **Oh no! He's coming! ...**

1 What? ... Yes. I wore a white dress. ... No. I can't send you
2 pictures! Look, Mummy, I've got to go! Just send someone to
3 help me, OK?

Dora's Dating Service

1 (As if giving a seminar) **All right, girls! This is the night**
2 **you've been waiting for! No more waiting by the phone,**
3 **checking your e-mail every hour, calling yourself to make sure**
4 **your phone is working! Those lonely nights are gone forever!**

5 I'm going to give it to you straight. Tell it like it is,
6 girlfriend to girlfriend, and when I'm done, you'll be on your
7 way to matrimonial bliss! That's right! You heard me. I'm
8 going to help you hook that man once and for all!

9 *And* I'm going to do it in just *three* easy steps! You heard
10 me right. *Three!* Believe me, you put these steps in action and
11 you'll be asking yourself how it could really be this easy!

12 Here we go! Step number one: Never appear smarter than
13 the man you want to catch. I played this one up like you
14 wouldn't believe! Acted like I couldn't even remember what I
15 was talking about. Just stopped mid-sentence and said,
16 "Where am I?"

17 I'm telling you girls, he couldn't figure it out! And let me
18 give you a little hint here, ladies! Every man likes a challenge!
19 You know how it is normally — you can barely get a "hello."
20 Well, you just throw a little confusion in the mix and he'll be
21 tripping over himself to talk to you. You'll be a puzzle that he
22 just can't figure out!

23 Step number two: Acting helpless will make a man want
24 to protect you. This little trick can take some acting, so you
25 may want to practice. I went for the whole "stung by a
26 jellyfish routine" ... like I'd really be dumb enough to touch
27 the tentacles! He bought it hook, line, and sinker! Believe me,
28 you just have to use the right bait to worm your way into your
29 man's heart.

Last but not least, step number three: Acting uninterested will hook them faster than you can say, "I do!" I asked my man, Marvin, what his name was at least *three* different times! In fact, I acted like I couldn't even remember *meeting* him! You should've seen his face! No man likes to be forgotten! After that, he wouldn't leave me alone! Followed me all over the ocean! We've been married six months now.

That's it, ladies! You put Dora's three simple steps into action, and I guarantee you'll be married in no time!

Queen Without Heart

1   People just can't handle a strong woman leader. The
2   can't. You give one little "Off with their head!" command and
3   everyone's calling you names they would never *dare* call a
4   man. Oh, no! A man who spouts commands is strong
5   Powerful! Someone to be revered! A woman is just a plain old
6   ... witch.

7   It's so unfair! Don't you think I'd rather my husband do all
8   the dirty work? Of course I would. But look at him! He's a
9   sniveling idiot. He can barely cut his own steak, much less
10 chop off someone's head. His heart bleeds more than a
11 freshly-popped zit.

12 But of course everyone *loves* him. Every time I give a
13 sentence, he's right behind me, pardoning the blasted
14 criminal. Says they should get a trial *before* sentencing! It's
15 completely ludicrous. A complete waste of my time. I *know*
16 they're guilty. Otherwise, I wouldn't have arrested them in the
17 first place. Guilty as charged is how it's got to be.

18 Just once I wish *he'd* be the heavy. Take charge of things
19 and give me the day off. But you know what the fool would do?
20 He'd release every prisoner and stop enforcing all my rules.

21 Mark my words, one day off and my kingdom would be in
22 chaos. Like it or not, I'm the woman in charge. Can I help it
23 that our kingdom is full of dirty, rotten ... *(Pauses and looks
24 Stage Left.)* What?

25 Oh dear! I must run. Appears I've got a blonde in the
26 garden bothering my playing cards! You see, my day just
27 never ends!

28 *(Runs off yelling.)* Off with her head!

The Hopping Mad Little Red Hen

1   *(Acting very preachy)* **Whoever said, "Teach a man to fish**
2 **and he'll eat forever," never had these bozos for friends! For**
3 **weeks I've tried to get these idiots to learn how to make bread**
4 **— from scratch — but they've absolutely refused! Stuck their**
5 **noses up in the air like a little work was going to kill them.**

6   **And when I say from scratch, I mean *from scratch*. No**
7 **Betty Crocker pre-packaged ingredients. No "just add water."**
8 **No *pre-made* anything. I'm talking planting, cutting, threshing,**
9 **grinding, and baking the stinking thing! No short cuts here!**
10 **But would Dog, Cat, or Duck listen to me? Of course not.**
11 **They wanted to play — swim in the pond, run around the field**
12 **— anything but help me!**

13   **Don't they want to know the feeling of making something**
14 **from nothing? Taking a tiny little seed and transforming it into**
15 **a loaf of bread? It's every baker's masterpiece. A work of art**
16 **worth savoring! What could possibly be more important than**
17 **that?**

18   **Sure it's time consuming. But what's a few months of**
19 **waiting when you can have something as perfect as this? Look**
20 **at the golden brown top. Breathe in that warm, yeasty smell.**
21 **Each piece is like a slice of heaven. You can't get taste like**
22 **this from a box! This kind of excellence only comes from**
23 **blood, sweat, and tears.**

24   *(Pause)* **What?** *(Looks incredulous.)* **You're lying! You *did not*!**
25 **I don't believe you! You did *not* switch my loaf with yours.**
26 *(Shaking head)* **There is *no way* this bread came out of a box!**
27 *(Gives in a little.)* **Well, OK, maybe it *looks* as good as mine,**
28 **but there's no way it tastes even halfway as good …** *(Pause)*
29 **Yeah, I'll try your cardboard bread and then I'll tell you …**

1   *(Pantomimes eating a small piece)* **how** *absolutely* *wonderful* it

2   **is! Omigosh! I've wasted so much time! Duck, Cat, Dog! Let's**

3   **go swimming!**

Goosey Not Loosey

1 　　See what a little gossip can do? Turn a whole stinking
2 town into chaos! What kind of people actually believe that the
3 sky is falling? Well, I'll tell you what kind of people! The same
4 close-minded idiots that believe that just 'cause you kiss a
5 couple of boys you got loose lips!

6 　　*I'm* not the one with the loose lips! Obviously no one
7 around here has ever heard of the old motto, don't kiss and
8 tell. Somehow the whole town knows everyone I've ever locked
9 lips with! I bet I know who started it all, too. Ducky Lucky! He
10 thinks he's some kind of Casanova with a nickname like that,
11 but the only thing lucky about him right now is the fact that I
12 haven't actually pulverized his face!

13 　　It's not like I've even kissed that many guys. Definitely not
14 as many as I could have! I don't say yes to everyone, you
15 know. I mean, I may be a goose, but even *I* have my
16 standards. So what's the big deal if I've given out a few
17 harmless pecks? If this town didn't thrive on gossip, no one
18 would even care!

19 　　But they're paying for their rumor mill now, aren't they?
20 Spreading gossip from a stupid little chicken! It serves them
21 right! Maybe next time they'll think twice before they call
22 someone Goosey Loosey!

Ho-Hum Heidi

1   I'm bored out of my absolute mind. I can't even believe
2 this place. I knew I was coming to live with my grandfather —
3 which is bad enough — but I didn't know he lived in the hills
4 of nowhere. The only neighbors he has are goats!

5   How can they expect a teenage girl to live this way? Do
6 you know how hard it is to even get a signal on my cell phone?
7 I have to climb up the highest hill, hold the phone out as far
8 as I can, and shout to the person I'm trying to call, "*Can you*
9 *hear me now*?"

10   Who knows if they can hear me 'cause I sure can't hear
11 them. I've had so many dropped calls that have been credited
12 back to my account that I think they actually *owe me*
13 minutes!

14   Oh, and you want to hear something else just as utterly
15 fantastic? No cable. No dish. *Nothing*! Not even free channels!
16 Just a whole lot of white snow — which I've actually watched
17 some nights just because I'm about to lose my mind!

18   No Internet. No IMing. No Facebook or MySpace. There's
19 absolutely *no way* for me to get in touch with my friends. At
20 least no twenty-first century way! My grandfather says, "Write
21 a letter." Who the heck writes letters at my age? And even if
22 I did, by the time I hike it down the mountain and this podunk
23 town's post office picks it up and delivers it, my friends
24 wouldn't even remember me! They'd be like, "Dude, you know
25 anyone named Heidi?"

26   Isn't it bad enough that my parents died? Now I gotta be
27 punished this way! Isn't there something in the constitution
28 about cruel and unusual punishment? Of course, what can I
29 do about it? I can't even *call* somebody!

Alice in La-La Land

1   OK, guys and girls, listen up. I'm here to share an
2   important message, and I want you to pay real good attention.
3   And I don't mean fake it, like *I* used to when I was the one
4   sitting in the uncomfortable bleachers, glad that at least I had
5   gotten out of class. Don't look surprised. I know what you're
6   thinking. I used to be just like you.

7   I thought I was invincible. That nothing bad was going to
8   happen to me. I didn't listen either when my friends, teachers,
9   or, God forbid, *my parents* told me anything. And that's why
10 I'm standing here in front of you today. See, I've got a story
11 to tell. One heck of a story.

12   It all started out with a drink. One simple little gulp from
13 a bottle. A bottle I'd never seen before. Didn't know where it
14 came from. Or even what was in it. Didn't know if someone
15 had slipped something bad into it. Didn't know. And to be
16 quite honest ... I didn't care. I drank it. Desperate to see what
17 it would do. Desperate to find an answer.

18   That one drink almost ruined my life! Almost instantly, I
19 fell into this imaginary world of talking rabbits, disappearing
20 cats and people made of cards! Scariest of all was a Queen
21 that yelled at me, "Off with your head!" It was a never-ending
22 nightmare, and I couldn't escape. A delusion I believed to be
23 real. I don't know how many days I stayed like that. I had one
24 heck of a headache though when it was all done, I can tell you
25 that!

26   So listen to me when I say it's true that people can slip
27 bad stuff into your drink. Never leave your glass — not even
28 for a minute. Even that might not be enough! All it takes is a
29 little distraction and you won't even know it happened!

61

1   Trust me, even if you have to order your drink with a sippy
2   cup — your peace of mind will be worth it!

Princess Lei – Caught on Tape!

1   I think I'm going to vomit! I mean it, you might want to
2 just step back a little before I upchuck all over you! How could
3 this have happened? It's bad enough that my first kiss got
4 caught on tape, but did it have to be my own *brother*? I'm
5 never going to live this down! And no wonder! It's disgusting!

6   The paparazzi have finally snagged their top news story!
7 It's going to be all over the galaxy before you know it. By the
8 eleven o'clock news, Duke and I will be on every channel.
9 People will talk about us for ages. No one will remember all
10 the good that we've done. The evil that we've conquered. The
11 lives that we've saved. Oh, no. All they'll ever remember is
12 that one stupid kiss!

13   Couldn't someone have told us before now? Everyone
14 could see what was happening. The fighting. The flirting. How
15 could they let it go this far? Did they think it was funny?
16 Playing with our emotions this way? I've always wanted a
17 brother ... but not like this! Now I'll never be able to even look
18 him in the face. Heck, I won't be able to look *anyone* in the
19 face!

20   That's why I've got to destroy that hologram! I can't let
21 something like this get out! No one will ever believe that it was
22 an accident. That we didn't know we were related. They'll
23 think we're sick. A brother and sister in love! Oh, Duke, why'd
24 you have to be so darn cute?

Pansy Beautyhair –
Series of Unfortunate Dates

1 It's always the same. First date. Never a second. I used to
2 think there was something wrong with me. Maybe I was too
3 smart for any boy. But I've studied it from every angle, and I
4 believe the truth is quite obvious. It's not *me* who's running
5 off my dates — it's them! My whacked-out family!

6 There's my nerdy brother who won't stop pestering me
7 about bookish things that normal boys just don't care two
8 cents about. He's enough to get on anyone's last nerve. Then
9 there's my baby sister, who takes every opportunity to give
10 each date a little gnawing! That's right — she bites them! In
11 fact, she bites everything! But that's a whole other story.

12 But if the two of them aren't bad enough, there's my
13 "Uncle Creepy." Otherwise known as Count Otto. Up until
14 very recently, we'd never even heard of him! Now he's in
15 charge of us. He's a dreadful old man whose eyebrow — and
16 I do mean one — looks like a hairy caterpillar about to molt!
17 He would scare even the bravest boy away!

18 The few times I've actually made it out of the house with
19 a boy, the Count is always lurking about. Popping up wherever
20 we are as if to make clear that he isn't about to take his evil
21 eyes off me. Sometimes I think that *he* wants to date me! Of
22 course I wouldn't put anything past him. He's been trying to
23 get his hands on our inheritance ever since our parents died.

24 So you can see that I'm destined to be single. You'd have
25 to be a weirdo to want to be around a family like mine ... and
26 who wants to date a weirdo?

Cruella DeMille, Puppy Rescuer

1 You'd never believe the way those poor puppies were
2 living! Cramped into a tiny apartment with no space to run
3 and play. They were practically tripping all over each other. I
4 couldn't let them live in conditions like that. *Some people* can
5 turn their head at such atrocities but not a *tender heart* like
6 me! I wouldn't have been able to sleep at night!

7 I just can't believe that Anna is a puppy hoarder! She sure
8 had the fur pulled over my eyes. Her loser husband, Robert,
9 probably talked her into it. It's obvious he's a moron who
10 can't land a real job — what is he, anyway? A writer of some
11 sort? What kind of man tries to support a family on pitiful
12 wages like that? No wonder he had to buy and sell puppies on
13 the side!

14 My darling Anna looked so sweet and innocent, too. I
15 guess that just goes to show how you can't judge a book by
16 its cover. Like me. All the time people think I'm some kind of
17 monster. Just because of this white streak that I've had since
18 birth. Does it matter that it's some kind of pigment issue? Of
19 course not. I've tried to dye the wretched streak, but the color
20 just washes right out. Believe me, I wouldn't look this way on
21 purpose. I look like a skunk is living on my head!

22 Now I'm the one being charged with puppy snatching ...
23 well, I *did* snatch the poor dears! But I wasn't going to hurt
24 them! I was trying to save them from the filth they were living
25 in. I'm not evil! I'm a hero! It's just not fair that I'll go to
26 bloody prison while Anna and Robert will get off scot-free.
27 They'll probably even get the puppies back!

28 Well, I won't give up! As soon as I'm out of here, I'll be
29 back! I'll be back to get you, my darling puppies!

Frozen-Faced Ice Princess

1   Somebody better find me a lawyer and find me one now!
2 That doctor will never work in Narnia again! I'm going to hit
3 him with a malpractice suit that will make his head spin. Take
4 him for everything he's got!

5   Just look what he's done to me! Look at my face! It's
6 frozen so tight I can't even smile! It hurts to even move my
7 mouth to speak. How am I going to eat? I can barely open my
8 lips far enough to breathe!

9   All I wanted was a little firming. A tad of Botox to take up
10 a few of the wrinkles. I'm not getting any younger, you know.
11 Lots of princesses have it done, and they look great! How was
12 I to know he could ruin my face forever? He promised me
13 youth and beauty — not this frozen ice cube of a face! No
14 wonder I heard people whispering when I walked into the
15 palace! I'm sure I heard someone call me the "Ice Princess."

16   If that's not bad enough, I heard there are some kids
17 nosing around in the kingdom. I don't have time to deal with
18 such nonsense. This is *not* the time to worry about fulfilling
19 some sort of prophecy nonsense! With a face like this, they
20 won't even take me seriously.

21   *(Pauses and pantomimes looking in mirror.)* Unless ... well, it
22 does look kind of scary, doesn't it? Almost like I'm made of
23 glass. Stiff. Frozen. Unemotional. Maybe I could use it to my
24 advantage. Scare off a couple of interfering kids ... and a
25 traitorous faun. I guess it won't be all that bad. I'll just have
26 to get used to eating from a straw!

Not-So-Humble Heroine

1   Larry this and Larry that. I'm sick to death of everything
2 being all about *him*. He's not even all that good of a wizard. I
3 can beat him in any spell any day of the week! Heck, I'm the
4 one who usually teaches him the spells in the first place. If it
5 weren't for me, Larry would've failed Spell Casting last year.
6 And the year before that. He's actually quite inept at
7 everything! He looks more like a nerd than a powerful wizard!

8   It's just as they say: Behind every great man, there's a
9 great woman! Absolutely true. I'm twice the wizard he is! Even
10 the teachers here at Bogwarts think so. You can tell they're all
11 quite sick of Mr. Lightning Bolt Head. So he got caught in the
12 crossfire of He Who Should Not be Named. Larry was a
13 stinking baby at the time. It's not like he's a hero or anything!

14   He struts around here — star of the Squidditch team —
15 like he's somebody. Well, without me, he'd be a nobody! He'd
16 be taking Spell Casting One-Oh-One, looking like a moron!

17   But even after all I've done for him, do you think he'd do
18 one little thing for me? No. I just want him to get Rob to like
19 me. Slip him a little love potion if he has to. Stupid Larry
20 refuses! Says he can't betray a friend that way! Well, what
21 about how he's betraying me? Taking advantage of my talents
22 and then taking credit for them?

23   Well, I'm done. Done being a doormat for Larry to wipe his
24 grimy little feet on. Just wait until he comes to me for help!
25 I'll tell him that he can use that fancy broom of his to fly
26 himself over to the library to research his own spells! I've got
27 better things to do!

SECTION 2

MONOLOGS FOR GUYS

The Clueless Leprechaun

1   (In an Irish accent, if possible) I don't understand why
2   everyone is always chasing me. Under bushes, through hollow
3   logs, up trees ... why can't they just leave me alone? I thought
4   all this green would disguise me, but it doesn't. And I'm a
5   really good hider. Even though I'm not that tall, they still find
6   me! Why? Why are they after me? I'm just a short little guy
7   that doesn't bother anyone ...

8   Well, I do pull some tricks every now and then, but that's
9   only because I get bored sometimes. But I'm harmless. Really.
10 Silly tricks like a dollar on a string. Or wet paint on a bench.
11 No biggies. Certainly not enough to warrant such a manhunt!
12 Why can't they leave me alone?

13   They even made up a day to celebrate me, yet do they ever
14 invite me to it? No way. I see them partying, wearing green,
15 drinking their green drinks, and having a good time. Even got
16 buttons that say, "Kiss me, I'm Irish!" When half of 'em ain't
17 never *been* to blimey Ireland much less been born there! It
18 burns my bum, I tell you.

19   It's always worse when there's a rainbow! The whole world
20 goes stark crazy. I have to scurry and hide. Like a scraggly old
21 dog or a rabbit on the run. What do they want with me? What
22 do they think I'm hiding? And what the dickens is a pot o'
23 gold anyhow?

The Paranoid Boogeyman

1   I know I shouldn't be telling you this, but I am so … sc
2 scared of the dark. I thought little kids were, too, but they're
3 not! Do you know how many children sleep in the dark these
4 days? The total dark? Not even a sliver of light! What are they
5 thinking? Don't they know how scary it is?

6   During the day I sneak in and hide, usually under the bed
7 because that's where it feels safe. I take a little nap. Get
8 settled in for the night, and then here come the kids. Loud
9 and whiny, "Do I *have* to go to bed?" the little monsters say
10 Then they get up a million times … potty … drink … just to
11 tell Mommy or Daddy goodnight again … on and on it goes
12 How am I supposed to get any sleep with all that racket?

13   Sometimes there's even jumping. *On the bed*! I have to
14 scrunch down real tight to the floor or my head gets thumped
15 It's not a fun night! Who's in charge here? The parents or the
16 kids, that's what I'd like to know.

17   Then comes the worst part. Total darkness. Out goes the
18 light. The door shuts, and the kid is left in there all alone! In
19 the dark! Well, not really alone because I'm there! But they
20 don't know that! Although sometimes they do look for me. A
21 quick peek in the closet or under the bed. But they never see
22 me because I'm good at hiding.

23   But I see them! And their beady little eyes scare me
24 Glowing in the dark like a green-eyed monster! It's no wonder
25 I stay under the bed! It's a scary world out there!

Randolph the
Dead-Nosed Reindeer

1   Just my luck. I finally get used to the stupid thing, and
2   bam. Out goes the light. Like somebody flipped the switch. I
3   had to do something. Can you imagine someone seeing me
4   like that? Normal? What would happen then? I'd go from being
5   extraordinary like Rudolph to being ordinary in half a second
6   flat.

7   Luckily, I had some neon-red paint left over from an
8   ornament I painted. I dabbed some of it on my nose. It'll work
9   for now, but I don't have much time. I gotta figure out how to
10 turn the thing back *on*! It's like my *signature*. I can't go back
11 to being a normal reindeer. It took too long to get this look to
12 work for me!

13   Like Rudolph, almost all my life I've been the butt of
14 everyone's jokes. Especially at first. I was an outcast! A freak
15 of nature! Another living, breathing, walking light bulb, for
16 Pete's sake! Everyone laughed at me.

17   No matter where I went, everyone knew where I was going.
18 Every day. There was pointing. And whispering. Nobody even
19 tried to hide it!

20   Sometimes I'd hear things like, "Well, I have an antler with
21 an extra nub," or "Look at how white my tail is; I stand out
22 like a sore thumb!" I don't know if they were trying to make
23 me feel better or make themselves feel more unique! But
24 nobody stood out as much as me! I was a walking nightlight!
25 How could anyone ever beat that?

26   After awhile I was almost a celebrity. I got almost as much
27 attention as Rudolph. My nose was a real attention getter! I
28 even got to lead the sleigh once. Number two reindeer —
29 that's me! Or was me ... See, without the nose, I got nothing!

1   I gotta get this thing fixed! And fast. It's just not fair that one
2   stinking "light bulb" goes out and I'm back to being a nobody.

The Ugly Duckling

1   My mother must be loose as a goose! No telling who my
2   real father is! I mean, look at me! Did she honestly think she
3   could get away with this? That no one would notice how
4   absolutely different I am from my brothers and sisters? I look
5   like a whole other species for crying out loud!

6   I blend in about as much as a fox in a herd of sheep.
7   What's my father going to say when he sees the family photo?
8   He'll end his tour of duty faster than you can say
9   "illegitimate!"

10   It'd take an idiot not to notice! Look at them, all sleek and
11   beautiful. Never a ruffled feather. Then look at me. I'm like a
12   storm cloud in the midst of a puffy white sky!

13   How could she do this to me? To him? I know Dad goes
14   away sometimes … maybe even a little longer than he should
15   — *obviously* — but this is *unforgivable*!

16   I wonder who my *real* dad is … the farmer's prize duck?
17   Or maybe that redneck guy that's always dropping by the
18   pond … chewing lazily on the grass, like he hasn't got a care
19   in the world … that's it! It's gotta be him! You just wait until
20   my father gets home! He'll tear the feathers off of him!

The Lonely Captain Hook

1   I know you won't believe this, but I actually care about that
2 silly boy named Peter. Without him, my ship would be in
3 shambles! Whenever the crew gets cabin fever and start beating
4 up on each other, here comes Peter, flitting about trying to cause
5 trouble. He thinks he's annoying me, but he's really helping me
6 out!

7   It's like cat and mouse. He plays tricks on my crew and me,
8 and we try to catch him. Well, they do. For me, it's all an act. I
9 have no interest in hurting the little booger. He's the only thing
10 exciting around here!

11   Do you know what it's like being stuck out to sea, seeing
12 nothin' but water for ages? It makes my sea legs quite wobbly, I
13 tell you! *(Staggers a bit.)* **And that ain't from the rum neither! Ha**
14 **ha!**

15   No, I've been riding that ol' wooden bucket for months. Hiding
16 out from the law. Floating along on the waves. Some days are real
17 exciting, like when we're looting or fighting. Other times are just
18 plain boring. Hanging out with a bunch of sweaty old men who
19 haven't bathed since the last time we saw land! It ain't a life for
20 the weak at heart, I can tell you that!

21   So it ain't no wonder I actually look forward to seeing Peter
22 flying around my ship, free as a bird. All dressed in green with that
23 silly pointed hat! Playing tricks on my crew and tangling up my
24 sails! Taunting us.

25   I'd have that little pipsqueak if I wanted. I would. But I can't
26 take away the crew's excitement. Oh look! Here he comes now!

27   "I'm gonna get you! You and that pixie bug! By hand or by
28 hook, I'm gonna get you!" *(As an aside in a whisper)* **The crew loves**
29 **it when I say that!**

Pig Genius: The Third Little Pig

1   My brothers are so dumb! Building houses out of straw
2   and sticks! *I* could even blow them down, and I've been
3   battling asthma since I was a piglet! What were they thinking?
4   Why even bother to build something if you're going to build
5   something so shabby! A complete waste of time and money!
6   And then, all that partying! Dancing that stupid jig like
7   they didn't have a care in the world! Eating like pigs, living
8   high on the hog! I doubt their combined IQ is bigger than a
9   gnat's! They almost deserve to get eaten by the big bad wolf!
10 Now, here they come crying, "Help us, help us!" Do they really
11 think he can't see them underneath that quilt?
12   As if he can't see two fat pigs in a blanket!
13   Well, where's the party now, I ask you? More importantly,
14 where were they when I was sweating like a pig laying all that
15 brick? Rolling in the mud, I'd say! Why should I let them lead
16 the wolf straight to me? It's them he wants!
17   Look at them run!   Listen to them squeal! It's almost
18 better than the Sunday night movie. Action. Suspense. Blood
19 and gore ...
20   Oh, I won't really let the wolf eat them! I promise. But
21 maybe I'll let him get a little nibble just to teach my brothers
22 a lesson! Houses of straw! It makes my tail curl!

The Completely Sane Emperor

1   Can you keep a secret? *(Puts hands to mouth like*
2 *whispering.)* I think I've lost my mind — you know, gone stark
3 raving mad! Crazy! Cuckoo. Call the looney bin!

4   See, everyone keeps telling me how wonderful I look in my
5 newly made clothes, and I think ... *(Again, hands to mouth)* I
6 think — I'm naked! Right down to my royal underwear! I don't
7 see a dag-blasted thing on me! I don't!

8   But how can everyone else see me in clothes, and I don't
9 see a single thread? Why would they lie? They know I'd
10 behead them for sure. Besides, it's not like they want to see
11 me in my birthday suit! Believe me, royal flab is not a pretty
12 sight! I lost my six-pack years ago, and I've got more hair
13 than the royal dog!

14   So it must be me! Like maybe my mother didn't hug me
15 enough, or maybe I got dropped out the palace window or
16 something! Or maybe my crown is too tight! There has to be
17 a reason. Everyone else can't be crazy ... can they?

18   But why can't I see my clothes? It doesn't make sense. I
19 get so confused! When I go to take a bath, I don't know
20 whether I'm naked or dressed! I can't tell if my clothes are
21 dirty or clean, or if I spilled soup down my front. What if I look
22 like a dirty pig and don't even know it?

23   I stare and stare at myself trying to see something. But all
24 I see is skin. How can this be happening? It's highly
25 upsetting. I think somebody better bring me a couch. I need
26 a visit with the Royal Psychiatrist!

Pinocchio and the Crooked Cricket

1   I don't know about you, but I don't like taking advice from
2 a bug! Everywhere I go, there's this cricket following me
3 around saying, *(Mocking)* "Don't do this. Don't do that." Who
4 is he to tell me what to do? He's as big as my toe, and I have
5 to listen to him? It doesn't even make any sense because
6 what does a bug even know about being a boy?

7   Sometimes I think he tells me to do the wrong thing on
8 purpose. You don't believe me? Well, it's true! I've seen him
9 laughing at me. He likes watching my nose grow. Yes, you
10 heard that right. My nose grows!

11   See, I've got this horrible affliction! Oh, I look all normal
12 now, don't I? A cute little boy made of wood. OK, OK, maybe
13 that's not so normal. But I can live with that. I've been that
14 way all my life, after all.

15   The real problem is that every time I tell a little fib — even
16 the tiniest little white lie, or even if I just stretch the truth a
17 wee bit — my nose sprouts out like a fast-growing weed!
18 Straight out from my face like a clothesline! Do you have any
19 idea how hard it is to walk around that way? I can't tell you
20 how many times I've poked someone in the eye or got my nose
21 shut in a door! It's downright embarrassing! As if having a
22 bug follow you around day and night wasn't bad enough.

23   Why me, I ask you. I can't possibly be the only boy to
24 stretch the truth a bit! How am I supposed to live with such
25 a wretched curse? How?

26   *(Pause)* What? Don't lie? I suppose that sounds all well and
27 good but … I'm just a little boy! You might as well cut my
28 strings and leave me here in a pile!

Jimmy the Unlucky Cricket

1   I've been seriously demoted. Made one little mistake, and
2   bam! I'm stuck watching some kid made of wood whose nose
3   sprouts faster than a dandelion weed on a freshly-mowed
4   lawn. When did I become a babysitter? Conscience to a piece
5   of carved lumber? Do I care if he makes the right decision?
6   No!

7   Eat the stolen cookie, play in the mud puddle, say the
8   stinking bad words — whatever. I mean, come on, the kid's
9   nose grows when he's bad. Does he really need *me* for
10 anything? Can't he figure it out on his own? Duh ... let's see.
11 I told a lie ... my nose grew ... maybe I shouldn't do that
12 again! I think he can get it! And if he can't, well then, hello!
13 He shouldn't get to be a real, live boy. This is the real world,
14 kid. You make choices. You pay the price.

15   Like me. I used to be a lucky cricket. Carried around like
16 a precious commodity. Treated like a king. Heck, I *lived* with
17 kings! Helped them win wars. Now look at me, jumping
18 around after a toothpick kid that wants to be a real boy. All
19 because of one little battle gone bad. Hey, no cricket can be
20 lucky twenty-four seven. Even the best have an off day! But
21 did I get another chance? *No!*

22   So let the pseudo-boy stay made of wood. If he can't
23 figure out the difference between right and wrong, that's *his*
24 problem. Besides, what real boys know the difference?

25   All I know is, I am a *lucky cricket.* I am *not* a *puppet*
26 *nanny.*

Not-So-Jolly Santa Claus

1   "Gimme! Gimme! Gimme!" "Wah, wah, wah!" Kids today
2 are so greedy! They want everything. Used to be I'd get one
3 toy, maybe two, on a list! Never more than three or four. Now
4 I get a two or three *page*, typewritten list, single-spaced,
5 sorted alphabetically. Sometimes it's even color-coded with a
6 legend and everything. Clearly marking all the items that are
7 "to die for."

8   I've never heard of such a thing. Toys that kids think they
9 can't live without. Cellphones, video games, electronic
10 gadgets that do everything but make their beds — which of
11 course they would never dream of doing anyway — believe me,
12 I see their rooms!

13   Things these days aren't cheap either! Half the stuff I've
14 never even heard of. There are gadgets *for* the gadgets, and I
15 swear I don't know what half of them do! How am I supposed
16 to give in to all these demands? I can't even fit all this stuff
17 on my sleigh! Do you know how many trips it would take to
18 give these kids everything they want?

19   My elves are exhausted. They've been hunting down toys
20 for months! Surfing the Internet. Shopping on Ebay. Putting
21 in bid after bid only to lose the auction at the last minute. It's
22 so frustrating!

23   Long gone are the days of toy making! We're not an
24 electronics factory, you know! No one wants a nice handmade
25 wooden train or hand-sewn dolly any more! These kids have
26 more things to plug in than I have in my whole workshop.

27   There's really only one thing to do. I'm going to have to get
28 pickier about my naughty and nice list. Obviously, I've been
29 letting a little too much slide by! These kids are getting

1   downright spoiled. Well, this year's going to be different. With
2   lists like these, those boys and girls are going to have to be
3   perfect angels!

The Frog Prince
of the Bachelor Pad

1   There I was, happy as a ... well, as a *frog*, I'd say! Not
2   bothering anyone. Certainly not wanting — or asking —
3   anyone to pick me up and ... and *kiss me*! *Aaaahhh!!!*
4   Who in their right mind goes around kissing frogs,
5   anyhow? Aren't there enough guys around the palace?
6   Couldn't she have left me alone? Oh, no! She had to pick me!
7   The innocent frog on the lily pad!
8   And now *look at me*! I'm a man — a *prince*! What do I
9   know about being a prince? I've been a frog for as long as I
10   can remember! And kissing girls? *Ewww!* Girls have cooties,
11   don't you know! I might even get warts! I've heard you get
12   those from humans, you know!
13   Why, oh why, couldn't I have stayed on my lily pad back
14   at the pond, basking in the sun, having day after glorious lazy
15   day! Now I have duties and responsibilities ... and clothes!
16   Hey! I know! Maybe if I kiss her again I'll change back!
17   Yeah, that's the ticket! OK ... here goes ... maybe I'll just hold
18   my nose ... *(Leans in holding nose.)* Oh, forget it! I'll just be a
19   stinking prince the rest of my life!

The Unwelcome Giant

1   Do you know how hard it is to find a size eighty shoe?
2 Well, it's nigh impossible, I tell you! Look what I'm wearing
3 now! Canoes! *(Lifts up foot.)* You can imagine how comfortable
4 that is! *(Sarcastic)* I've got more splinters than a piece of
5 wood! When these fall apart I don't know what I'll wear! It's
6 not like there's an unlimited supply of canoes around here.
7 And it's getting far too cold to go barefoot!
8   Clothes aren't any better. I've been wearing this tent now
9 for three months! Oh, it's great in the rain — waterproof and
10 all — but man, is it hot in the sun! I swear I've sweated off
11 twenty pounds! So much in fact, I started a new little river!
12 Ha ha.
13   That sure made the little people scamper! Like a bunch of
14 ants, they are! I bet they don't have any trouble finding wee
15 little clothes and shoes! They're so small, I can barely even
16 see them! Which isn't good, I can tell you. I didn't mean to
17 squash a few. I didn't. But do you think they'd believe me?
18   Oh, no. They go running and screaming every time they
19 see me coming. Which is *all* the time, because of course they
20 can spot me from about a mile away! I'm as tall as a tree, for
21 crying out loud! In fact, I'm taller than half the forest! They
22 think I'm some sort of monster just 'cause I'm bigger than
23 they are. I don't know why they can't just leave me be.
24   They're always setting traps for me. Digging big holes,
25 stringing up ropes. Makes it hard to have any peace and
26 quiet. It's not like I have any place I can hide, either. When
27 you're taller than the trees, there aren't many places to go. I
28 can't even find shade, much less a hiding spot. I'm always
29 stuck out in the sun, burning the tips of my ears and the top

1   of my head.

2   I just wish I could shrink down a wee bit — maybe not as

3   tiny as those little munchkins — but small enough to get out

4   of the sun and put my feet in something other than a boat!

The Fed-Up Genie

1   Poof! Give me what I want! Poof! Give me what I want! Poof!
2 Give me what I want! That's how it goes all day long! I don't ever
3 get a minute's peace! It's like I was *born* to serve them! Well, I
4 have a life too, you know!

5   There I'll be, taking a bath, reading a book, talking to my
6 mama — anything — when, bam! Someone's gotta rub the lamp,
7 and out I come like a puff of smoke! No apology, no "Sorry for
8 disturbing you," no "Is this a good time?" Nothing! Just *gimme,*
9 *gimme, gimme*! It's all about them and their greedy little wishes!

10   Half the time they don't even know what they want! Not
11 because they don't want anything — oh, no! — but because they
12 can't narrow it down to three! They forget that just minutes before
13 they weren't going to get *anything*! And now they want it all.

14   Seems like everyone tries the whole "Can I wish for another
15 three wishes?" gag. Do they really think that's going to work?
16 Come on. Do I *look* like a moron?

17   Well, OK, maybe I look a little silly in this stupid genie suit,
18 but it comes with the job. Believe me, I didn't pick it out. I look
19 like M.C. Hammer in his old poofy pants days! They didn't look
20 good on him, and they sure don't look good on me. The fat just
21 looks fatter, if you know what I mean.

22   But back to the people. *Three wishes!* Uno. Dos. Tres. It's not
23 that hard. They stand there throwing things out, and when I get
24 ready to give them their wish, they say, "I didn't actually wish for
25 that. I was just thinking." Well, think a little faster, people! I don't
26 have all day to watch you "eenie, meanie, minie, mo" your
27 choices!

28   Get a clue! Know what you want *before* you rub the lamp!

Aladdin's Real Wish

1   All day long it's the same. Poof! What do you want? Poof!
2   What do you want! Can't you see that I just *want* to be left
3   alone? I don't need you popping up out of nowhere asking me
4   about stupid wishes. If I *knew* what to wish for, I would've
5   done it already.

6   Thing is, I don't even *want* the stupid wishes. I've seen
7   what happens to people who all of a sudden get everything
8   they want. Those big-time lottery winners who say, "This
9   won't change my life at all." And then they go completely off
10   the deep end. Buy everything they can think of, and in the end
11   they wind up losing *everything*. Every last dime, and then
12   some! They might as well have never won the lottery, if you
13   ask me.

14   Same thing here. I'm not stupid. I know what they say
15   about, "If it sounds too good to be true, then it is." What
16   could sound better than all of a sudden being granted three
17   wishes for doing absolutely nothing besides rubbing the dust
18   off a dirty old lamp? There's bound to be a catch in there
19   somewhere.

20   Don't shake your head, Genie. I know you got something
21   up your sleeve. Like maybe I'll be giving my soul to the devil
22   or something. Or ... I know! I'll get sucked down in that lamp
23   and have to stay there. And you'll get to go free! That's it,
24   isn't it? You're the last sucker that bought into that whole
25   "three wishes" deal, and now you're stuck! Trapped in that
26   little bitty bottle for all of eternity!

27   Well, ha ha! You're gonna stay in there if it's up to me. I
28   don't need your wishes! I'll change my life around on my own,
29   thank you very much. A little hard work and determination,

1   and one day I'll be living it up at the palace. You'll see. I don't
2   need some overstuffed genie working his magic in my life. So
3   Genie, you can just pop yourself back into that bottle 'cause
4   I am *not* making any wishes!

Overtime Elf

1   All work and no play makes for a very busy day! And night!
2   Where's social services, I'd like to know. Aren't there any labor
3   laws to protect us? We need a Toy Makers' Union, that's what we
4   need. They can't expect us to work all the time and never have
5   any fun. It's unconstitutional!
6   And look at that! *(Pantomimes pointing out a window.)* **All that**
7   snow and we're stuck in here making toys! I want to build a
8   snowman, have a snowball fight, make a snow angel! Or, better
9   yet, go sledding! I mean look at those hills! They're begging for a
10   sleigh ride!
11   Instead we're stuck in here. Making toys. It's not that I don't
12   love my job. I do. Especially since I'm in Quality Control. I get to
13   test all the toys, and that can be a lot of fun. But everyone needs
14   — and *deserves* — a break every now and then! Nobody should
15   have to work twenty-four seven! We're elves, not *robots*, for crying
16   out loud!
17   Not only do we work day and night, we have to do it in these
18   silly little uniforms and pointed shoes! Don't even get me started
19   on that! Why does it matter what we wear? No one sees us! We're
20   not allowed any visitors. It's the same old faces day in and day
21   out. It's like we're in our own little world. I don't know if people
22   know we really exist out here in the middle of nowhere.
23   *(Turns as if hearing a sound.)* **Darn. There goes the whistle. Our**
24   two-and-a-half-minute cocoa break is over. I guess I'd better get
25   back to work. I don't want to make you-know-who mad! You think
26   he's all jolly, but you just wait until you make him upset! Last
27   week he sent someone to live with the Abominable Snowman!
28   *(Pauses.)* **Hey, I wonder if *he* has any fun?**

Tootin' Jack and the Beans

1   I thought Mother would be so proud of me! My very first
2 trip to the market, and I made a fabulous trade! Beans for a
3 stupid old half-starved goat! I couldn't believe my luck.

4   I didn't really believe the man who said they were magical.
5 Just figured they'd make for a good crop once I planted them.
6 Then we'd never go hungry again. Mama can make a mean
7 bean soup, and I knew she'd be happy that I'd gotten such a
8 good deal.

9   On the way home, I couldn't help but be a little curious,
10 though. What if those beans really were magical? I knew they
11 weren't, but just in case ... I thought it wouldn't hurt to try
12 one or two.

13   They really didn't taste any different. Just like regular
14 beans, only a little more sour. I kept walking, thinking I was
15 pretty silly for even thinking for a second about what that man
16 had said. But then I got a bubbly feeling inside me, and my
17 stomach swelled to the size of a turnip. By the time I got near
18 the house, my tummy was near as big as a watermelon!

19   I couldn't believe my luck! They really were magical.
20 Magical growing beans. I rushed into the house, anxious to
21 see the look on my mother's face when I showed her the bag
22 of beans. Oh, I knew they didn't look like much ... but that
23 was to be expected! Obviously you couldn't have magic beans
24 looking all magic-like or *everybody* would want them! They
25 had to look ordinary! It took me awhile to explain that to
26 Mama.

27   Then, it happened. All that "magic" started to come out
28 ... now don't ask how 'cause I surely can't tell you that. *(Looks
29 sheepish.)* It's downright embarrassing. And not very polite.

1 Mama laughed and laughed and said she had a fool boy for a
2 son. Then she made me go out back. Number one: To plant
3 those stupid beans, and number two: To get me out of the
4 house. She said, "Maybe those beans *are* magic, Jack, 'cause
5 they go in smelling like beans and come out smelling like ..."
6   Well, I can't really tell you the rest of what she said. All I
7 know is I'll never eat another bean for as long as I live!

The Big Bad Wolf
and His Sick Sense of Humor

1   Whoa! Hold back on the axe, man! This is all a big
2 mistake! It was a joke! An innocent prank gone wrong. I
3 wasn't going to eat her! I promise! I'm a vegetarian. Gave up
4 meat two weeks ago. In fact, I'm more like a vegan. I don't
5 even eat anything that's been anywhere near meat. Especially
6 fresh young meat like her. I swear. I wasn't going to harm a
7 hair on her hooded head.

8   But a wolf's got to have some fun, you know? That's all it
9 was. A little fun. You should've seen her face!

10   *(Mocking)* "Why Grandma, what big teeth you've got!" Was
11 she for real? The girl needs some serious glasses if she really
12 thought I was her grandma. Look at all the fur, man! *(Points*
13 *at arm.)* Don't you think she should've had a clue? I mean, if
14 her grandma looks like this, then she's got one freaky
15 grandma!

16   Whoa! Back up a little! Is it my fault the girl can't see? I
17 thought she'd take one look at me and run laughing — or
18 screaming — from the room! I never dreamed she'd stick
19 around. Know what she did? She practically stuck her head in
20 my mouth; she was so close to my face! You gotta give me a
21 break, man! I couldn't help but lick her a little! But I wasn't
22 going to eat her, I swear! You've got to believe me!

23   Go check the closet! Her old granny's in there. I didn't
24 harm a gray hair on her head! Go on! Go see! *(Points in one*
25 *direction and then runs Off in the other direction.)*

26   *(Yells.)* Some people just can't take a joke, can they?

Patch the Dragon

1   I'm so tired of the smell of smoke. Don't they have a patch
2 or something to help you stop smoking? Think they got one
3 big enough for me? 'Cause I'm ready to quit. I am.

4   Every time I find a nice, comfortable place to stay — you
5 know, a really deep, dark cave — it happens. One little
6 sneeze, and wham! The place goes up in smoke! I think it's
7 the dust or dirt that makes it happen, but how do you find a
8 place without dust? Especially a cave! And I can't help it that
9 I'm allergic! Believe me, I wish I wasn't!

10 Why does fire even come out of my snout? That's what I'd
11 like to know! No one else seems to have that problem. Not
12 one other animal in the forest sneezes fire! So why me?

13   I don't have any friends; nobody will come close to me. I
14 can't blame them, I guess. I wouldn't want to be fried to a
15 crisp either. It's bad enough that I'm the biggest animal in the
16 forest! I mean, you can definitely pick me out in a crowd! So
17 why do I have to breathe fire, too? How is that fair?

18   Do you know how lonely I get sitting around the forest all
19 day trying not to sneeze? It isn't fun, I can tell you that! I just
20 wish someone would like me for who I am. Fire and all. But
21 that's probably ... not ... going ... to ... *aaahhhchooo!* ...
22 happen, is it?

23   *(Puts hand to mouth.)* **Ooops** ... sorry ... you got a little fire
24 going there ... on your head.

Trading Spaces Tarzan

1 My hands are killing me! Look at them! *(Thrusts hands to*
2 *audience.)* Blisters on top of blisters! It's all this swinging from
3 place to place, I tell you! I'm not a monkey. I'm a man! But
4 walking takes forever, and then my *feet* get blisters! I need a
5 good pair of shoes. Or a pair of gloves! Not to mention a pair
6 of pants!

7 Do you know how drafty this loincloth gets? I feel like I'm
8 wearing a diaper! How am I supposed to look manly in this?
9 And I could use a little more coverage, if you know what I
10 mean! Half the jungle's seen my backside! And that's not a
11 pretty sight, let me tell you.

12 I gotta *live* in the trees, *swing* from the trees, *eat* from the
13 trees. I just can't take it any more! All this outdoor living. It's
14 the same old thing day in and day out. How much fresh air
15 can a person take? And fresh food isn't all it's cracked up to
16 be, either. Vegetables and fruit. Nuts and berries. Gag me.
17 What I really want is a burger and fries! Haven't I been out
18 here long enough?

19 Either I got to get out of here or someone's got to help me
20 turn this place around! A total change of space. Transform
21 this tree house into a real home. A place fit for the king of the
22 jungle. There has to be someone out there who could do
23 something with all of this!

24 Maybe *I* could even get a makeover. Haircut, new clothes.
25 Manicure and pedicure. Just 'cause I live like an animal
26 doesn't mean I have to look like one, right?

27 Well I've got to run — or rather, swing! I'll see you around
28 the jungle!

29 *(Does "Tarzan yell" as he exits.)*

The Boy Who Cried Wolf

1   You know how you'll be bopping along, minding your own
2 business, when all of a sudden something really incredible —
3 I mean, super spectacular — comes along? Like a triple
4 rainbow, or a glimpse of the Loch Ness monster, or maybe
5 even Big Foot crossing the road? And you try to get
6 someone's attention so they can see it, only they're too busy
7 to pay any attention to you and by the time they *decide* to look
8 up, that thing that you know you'll never see again in all your
9 life, is *long gone*?

10   Well, that's how it is with me. Only it's nothing wonderful
11 and spectacular. See, there's this wolf that's been harassing
12 me. Follows me everywhere I go. Always lurking. Waiting to
13 catch me unawares. Every time I catch a glimpse of him and
14 try to point him out to someone, he darts away. *Every darn*
15 *time*!

16   Everyone's started calling me a liar. Saying I'm making
17 things up to get attention. Worse, they say I'm seeing things.
18 That I'm so *paranoid* that I'm afraid of my own shadow! They
19 either think I'm a liar or a scaredy-cat. Absolutely no one will
20 take me seriously.

21   But why would I lie about something like this? Do I look
22 like someone who wants to get eaten by a wolf? What kind of
23 idiot would joke about something like that? Doggone it, when
24 I cry wolf, *I mean it*!

The Easter Chicken

1   *(Acting like a chicken)* **Bawk! Bawk! Bawk!** *(Stops chicken*
2   *act. Gets more and more worked up as monolog continues.)* **I can**
3   **see you think I'm crazy. But why shouldn't I squawk like a**
4   **stupid chicken? I mean, really, what does a bunny have to do**
5   **with a bunch of eggs? Whoever dreamed up something so**
6   **ridiculous? All I know is every year I fill Easter baskets with**
7   **candy, and maybe a small toy or two. Next day, instead of**
8   **pigging out on sugary sweets, those stinking kids are all**
9   **hunting for eggs. I'm serious! They leave their goody baskets**
10   **sitting around while they go off like a bunch of maniacs to find**
11   **stupid painted eggs.**

12   *Eggs!* **It's starting to tick me off. What kind of kid gets**
13   **excited about a bunch of hard-boiled eggs? Especially when I**
14   **leave them** *chocolate.* **And** *jelly beans.* **Has the world turned**
15   **upside down? No kid picks eggs over chocolate.**

16   **Where do all these eggs come from, anyway? It's like I got**
17   **a stalker chicken going around behind me messing up my gig.**

18   **The funniest thing is, everyone thinks they're mine.** *Hello!*
19   **Get a clue. Bunnies** *do not* **lay eggs! And we certainly don't**
20   **paint them and hide them. Why in the world would I have**
21   **anything to do with eggs? Carrots, maybe. Or lettuce. Maybe**
22   **even turnips. But eggs?**

23   **Let me just set the record straight, OK? Number one, I**
24   **am the Easter** *Bunny* **not** *Chicken.* **I do not** *lay* **eggs,** *paint*
25   **eggs,** *hide* **eggs, or even** *eat* **eggs. If all this craziness does not**
26   *stop,* **I will never leave jellybeans or chocolate in your baskets**
27   **ever again. You can pig out on hard-boiled eggs for all I care.**
28   **And maybe, if you're lucky, the Easter** *Chicken* **will bring you**
29   **a batch of** *chocolate eggs!* **But I wouldn't count on it, 'cause**

1   **guess what?** *(Has really gone off the deep end at this point.)*
2   *Chickens don't lay chocolate eggs!*

Arachnophobic Arachnid Man

1   Look at this place! It's a disaster! Webs are everywhere! In the
2   corners, up on the ceiling — I even had one in my bathtub this
3   morning! Do you know how gross that is? I could barely scrub
4   myself because I kept getting tangled up. This web mess is
5   getting out of control!

6   I know what you're thinking. Lousy housekeeper! Utter slob!
7   Well, I'm not! I'm actually quite the neat freak. These aren't
8   cobwebs. They're spider webs! Sticky, icky, totally annoying
9   spider webs! And no, I'm not some kook running an exotic spider
10   farm or something. I promise you that! I absolutely hate spiders!

11   So what's up? I'll tell you what's up! They come from *me*!
12   Right here out of my wrist. *(Holds up arm and points to wrist. Acts*
13   *like accidentally gets web on someone.)* **Ooops. Sorry. See? It**
14   happens all the time. I cough or sneeze, and bam! Out flies a web!
15   I have no idea how to control the silly things. I spend all day
16   knocking down webs and then they're right back up. It's a never-
17   ending job. And a sticky one, too.

18   Last night I got myself caught in one — like a fly in a trap —
19   I was wriggling around in that thing for hours. I even fell asleep in
20   there for a while — hanging upside down from the ceiling — I was
21   so exhausted from all the struggling.

22   Do you know what kind of nightmares one has when stuck in
23   a web? All night long I dreamed of red eyes and big fangs coming
24   to get me. It gives me chills just thinking about it!

25   If I could just figure out what I'm supposed to do with these
26   things. It's not like I'm wanting to catch a big bug or anything!
27   *Yuck!* So what good are they? Why am I like a human spider?

28   Aaaachooo! Oh man! There goes another one! I gotta go!

Acrophobic Super-Duper Man

1   It's an eagle. It's a jet. It's ... oh, give me a break.
2   Everyone knows it's me. But what I bet they don't know is
3   this: I absolutely hate flying. I do! It scares me to death. Being
4   way up there! Do you know how far down the ground is from
5   where I fly? A man could get seriously hurt if something went
6   wrong.

7   You think I don't consider that while I'm up there zipping
8   around? Well, I do. It's a long, long way down. That's why I
9   close my eyes sometimes, but do you know how many times
10   I've had to dodge a plane? Or a flock of geese? Believe me,
11   those birds aren't so nice when you upset their formation. I
12   can't tell you how many times I've been attacked! One day I'm
13   liable to get pecked to death, right up there in the sky.

14   I just wish I could stay grounded. Like man is supposed
15   to. But what choice do I have? When someone needs me, I
16   have to get there fast. There's no advance warning. No time
17   to hail a cab or hop on the subway! I'd be the laughingstock
18   of all superheroes if I did that!

19   I've thought about getting a car, but have you *seen* the
20   traffic around here? People drive like maniacs, too! I wonder
21   how many times the Batmobile's been wrecked! I couldn't
22   afford the insurance on something like that!

23   I guess, all in all, I'm safer in the air. It's kind of peaceful
24   ... up in the clouds ... *(Looks up at sky dreamily)* ... oh, who am
25   I kidding? It's terrifying! One of these days I've got to get a
26   new job! Like newspaper reporter or something!

Iron-Pumping Sockeye

1   I work and I work and I work. And for what? For a can of
2   *spinach* to take all the credit? You see these guns? *(Holds up*
3   *arms to show muscles.)* **These babies don't just happen**
4   **overnight, you know.**

5   Every morning I get up at five a.m. and go to the gym. I
6   pump iron for at least two hours. Then I swim a couple of
7   miles, and then I do the punching bag for about a half an
8   hour. It's no sissy routine, I can tell you that! If I thought a
9   can of spinach could do that, I'd buy it by the case. Heck, I'd
10   have acres and acres of the stuff. Who wouldn't? Why would I
11   work so hard if it were so easy?

12   I don't know who started that crazy rumor in the first
13   place. Probably the Jolly Green Giant. Trying to increase
14   sales. Telling little kids that if they "eat their spinach" they
15   can be strong and muscular like me! It's hilarious! Like telling
16   people if they "just take one of these pills a day" they can get
17   skinny! Or this makeup will make you look pretty. Or this
18   cream will make you grow hair!

19   Nobody would ever fall for anything that stupid, would
20   they? So why are they saying that about *me*? Making me look
21   like a vegetable-swigging moron!

22   *(Sarcastic, as if doing a commercial)* **Ooooh, look at me, I sit**
23   **around all day being fat and lazy, then whenever I want, I**
24   **guzzle a can of spinach, and whamo! I'm the world's strongest**
25   **man! It's that easy! No fuss. No mess.** *(Pantomimes holding up*
26   *a can of spinach.)* **Just eat it straight from the can. You don't**
27   **even have to heat it up. It's great hot or cold! Want to look**
28   **like me? Well, what are you waiting for? Grab that can of**
29   **spinach and pop the top! You'll be amazed at the results!**

Hemophobic Count Dracula

1　　You sleep in a coffin, and all of a sudden you're a monster?
2　Why? I don't sleep in there because I *have* to; I do it because
3　I *want* to. I'm not *afraid* of the light like everyone says. I just
4　prefer the dark. Always have. Even when I was little, I never
5　would use a nightlight. Always slept under a mound of covers.
6　I just got used to it. And as I got older I wanted it to be darker
7　and darker. Well, what's darker than a really good coffin, I ask
8　you? Nothing. Absolutely nothing. It's like being in a cave.
9　Completely glorious.

10　　And if them calling me a monster isn't bad enough, they
11　got to make up some ridiculous story about me drinking
12　people's blood. Number one: *Ewww*! How disgusting is that!
13　Number two: Look at me, I go pale at even the thought of
14　blood! That's right. I'm a hemophobe, through and through.
15　Don't look at me like I'm crazy! Lots of people are afraid of
16　blood. It's not *that* unusual. You should see me when they pull
17　out a needle. I hit the floor faster than you can say, "silver
18　bullet."

19　　I don't understand why everyone thinks that I sneak
20　around under the dark of night, doing these horrible,
21　unspeakable things. Truth is, a long time ago, I tried going
22　around during the day. But people were cruel. Laughed and
23　pointed. Didn't even try to hide it. Can I help it that I have
24　teeth like a saber-toothed tiger? It's not like I have a dental
25　plan or anything. I haven't had a job in years. If it weren't for
26　my parents' inheritance, I'd be out on the street.

27　　All I want is to be left alone. Well, that and a girlfriend,
28　maybe. But who would ever date me? I can just see it now.
29　Everyone would go crazy. Headlines as big as the sky: "Love

1   at First Bite. Dracula Falls in Love." I'm destined to be a
2   bachelor forever ... but then again, there's really no room in
3   the coffin!

Dr. Jekyll and Mr. Hyde: Separated at Birth

1   *(As if under interrogation)* **It wasn't me. I swear. I was at**
2   **home last night. Reading a book. Watching a little TV. I didn't**
3   **even leave the house. Not once. You've got to believe me. I**
4   **would never hurt someone that way ... please take those**
5   **pictures away ... they're making me sick. Who could do such**
6   **a thing?**
7   **Don't look at me that way! You're not even listening to**
8   **what I'm saying. I can see it in your eyes. You think I'm guilty.**
9   *Guilty as charged!* **Where's my lawyer? How can you keep me**
10 **here like this? Don't I have any rights? Can't I at least make**
11 **a phone call? I haven't done anything wrong! Where's the**
12 **justice around here? I'm** *innocent* **until** *proven* **guilty,**
13 **remember?**
14 **I'm a doctor, for heaven's sake. A well-respected member**
15 **of this community! This is a farce. While you're sitting here**
16 **with me, the** *real* **killer is walking around scot-free. You have**
17 **no reason to even suspect me! No proof of any kind ...** *(Pause,*
18 *as if being spoken to).*
19 **What?! That's impossible! I'm a scientist. You can't pull**
20 **these lies over on me! There is absolutely no way my DNA can**
21 **be on that knife! I've never even seen it before. Let me see**
22 **those papers ...** *(Pantomimes reading then dropping papers down.*
23 *Looks shocked.)* **You're sure? There's no mistake?**
24 *(Pause)* **Then it can only mean** *one* **thing. I have an**
25 **identical twin! Don't you see? That's the only logical**
26 **explanation. How else would someone have the same DNA!**
27 **Omigosh, this is impossible!** *(Excited)* **I've got a brother!** *(Not*
28 *so excited)* **And he's a murderer!**

Jack Sprat Could <u>Get</u> No Fat!

1   My wife is an absolute pig! She is! I'll see her cooking in
2 the kitchen, frying up something good, and my stomach will
3 get all jittery with excitement, thinking that I'm going to get
4 some good old fried chicken or maybe some hot buttery rolls.
5 But you know what she brings out for me? Salad. No dressing.
6 Or maybe some dried-up, *skinless* chicken with no flavor.

7   If I'm *really* lucky, I'll get something made with this junk
8 called tofu ... what the heck *is* that? I'll tell you what it isn't
9 — it is *not* meat! It may have protein, but it isn't anything like
10 sinking your teeth into a plump, juicy steak! Nothing at all!
11 It's some kind of nasty mush that my wife tries to tell me is
12 much *better than meat.* Well, if it's so good, why doesn't she
13 eat it?

14   "*You* have to watch your cholesterol, dear," she'll say.
15 "Thank the good Lord, my cholesterol is absolutely perfect."
16 Then she'll polish off a hamburger and fries faster than I can
17 even *say* cholesterol.

18   If she catches me eating anything that isn't lean, mean
19 and green, she'll snatch it away and say something like, "You
20 know you can't have that! Do you want to die? Do you?"

21   Well, guess what? Yes. Yes, I do! If all I've got to look
22 forward to is rabbit food for the rest of my life — why live it?
23 I'm sick of watching her eat all that greasy goodness while I
24 crunch myself to death on carrots!

25   Besides, just because her cholesterol is in the perfect
26 range doesn't mean she can lick the fried chicken bucket
27 clean! Her rear-end is getting as big as the house! We don't
28 even sleep in the same bed anymore! She says it's because I
29 snore, but it's really because she just about killed me! One

1 night she rolled over on me and I couldn't breathe. She broke
2 three of my ribs!
3   The doctor might say that I "can't eat no fat," but
4 somebody better tell my wife that she's got to eat some lean!

Sorcerer's Apprentice, a.k.a. the Big Guy's Servant

1   This is absolutely the worst job ever. Not at all like the
2 program I signed up for. *(Mimicking an advertisement)* "Learn
3 the ways of a famous wizard." "Go from apprentice to expert
4 in just six short months." "Want to take the fast track? Then
5 vocational training is for you!"

6   Well, this program is for you ... if you're a sucker! It's the
7 fast track to *nowhere*! I've been here three years already and
8 I still can't do anything more than a basic spell. Stuff I learned
9 back in kindergarten. I'm so busy doing all the cooking and
10 cleaning that I don't have any time to learn anything! I barely
11 even *see* the wizard, much less have any instruction from him.

12   I'd like to leave, but how would that look? I took a six-
13 month program for three years and *still* didn't graduate? I'd
14 look like a complete moron. I could've gotten my Bachelor's
15 of Wizardry by now!

16   I've tried to do some studying on my own. Cast my own
17 spells. Some of them have been quite good. I even turned a
18 stick into a snake. Of course the wizard didn't believe me
19 since it slithered away before I could show him.

20   He said I wasn't ready for "life-changing" spells, so I just
21 had to prove him wrong. Brought a couple of brooms and
22 some buckets to life. Only, things got out of hand. Really out
23 of hand! The stupid things were multiplying faster than a
24 couple of jack rabbits! Everything I tried just made things
25 worse!

26   When the Sorcerer got home, he had to clean it all up.
27 Well, if you call waving your wand and spouting some words
28 cleaning it up! He didn't even break a sweat. But it doesn't
29 matter. He hasn't let me forget it. Says he'll tell everyone how

1   incompetent I am if I even think about leaving now.
2   He thinks I'm his prisoner. His own little wizard-servant.
3   Well, wait 'til he finds out that I may not be learning anything
4   from him, but I'm getting really good at self-study!

Psychotic Dr. Bill

1   Wah. Wah. Wah. *(Mocking)* "I'm so pathetic." "I can't make
2 up my mind about anything." "I just need someone to tell me
3 what to do." "I'm too fat." "I'm too skinny." "I'm too rich."
4 "I'm too poor." "I'm too pretty." "I'm too ugly." "I'm too
5 busy." "I'm too lazy."
6   "Help me, Dr. Bill. Help me!"
7   Where do the producers find these stupid people? After all
8 these years, shouldn't we be running out of idiots? It's always
9 the same thing. Day in and day out. They mess up their lives
10 and then come crying to me to fix them!
11   "I spent fifty thousand dollars on shoes last year, Dr. Bill.
12 Was that wrong?"
13   "Dr. Bill, I went out with my sister's husband. Now I can't
14 sleep at night. Should I tell her?"
15   "We let our children stay up as late as they want, and now
16 they're falling asleep in school ... what should we do, Dr.
17 Bill?"
18   Has *no one* besides *me* ever heard of common sense? It's
19 not rocket science, people! Sometimes I think they pretend to
20 be dumb just to get on the show, but then I talk with them
21 ... and, no, they really are *that dumb*! It's amazing that some
22 of them can find the studio on their own!
23   The worst are the criers. I can't tell you how many times
24 I've hugged one of them only to find dried snot on my jacket
25 later! Not only are they pathetic, they can't even use a tissue?
26 Do they have any idea how much one of these suits costs?
27 More than they've ever spent on therapy, obviously! I tell you
28 one thing, there shouldn't be any psychiatrists out of a job
29 any time soon! I'm starting to wonder if there are any sane

1 people left in this world!
2   *(Pauses and acts like someone is gesturing for him.)* **Yeah. I'm**
3 **coming.** *(To audience)* **Well, I gotta go. The world can't seem to**
4 **go on without me.**

Bernie the
Color-Crazed Dinosaur

1   Can you say "Purple"? I thought you could. Now, can you
2   say, "Dinosaur"? I knew you could. Now let's put that
3   together, OK? "Purple dinosaur." OK, one last thing. Can you
4   say, "Crazy"? *I thought you could!* (*Gets really crazy, loud, and*
5   *angry.*)

6   A purple dinosaur! Who ever heard of such a thing?! It's
7   unbelievable! I can't even believe *my own eyes*! I look down,
8   and I'm like, "Whoa! Where's the green, dude?" It's like living
9   in a bad dream, and you can't wake up.

10   I remember being younger and noticing I was different, but
11   I just kept thinking that when I got older, I'd change colors.
12   Like all my dinosaur friends. But I didn't. If anything, I turned
13   deeper purple.

14   So then I thought that maybe if I surrounded myself with
15   green, like leaves and grass, I'd change colors like a
16   chameleon. Yeah. Well, *that* didn't work.

17   So then I thought that maybe if I got real jealous, you
18   know, of all the other *normal* dinosaurs, that I'd be green with
19   envy! Well, guess what, folks? That didn't work either!

20   After all that, I was pretty blue. (*Sarcastically*) Ha ha. I
21   mean, purple! I figured there was no way to change what I
22   was: a purple dinosaur. But you know what? I got used to all
23   that attention. Even landed this sweet television show. I
24   guess that's when I finally realized that it's OK to just be me.
25   Purple and all.

26   Can you say, "Unique"? Well, that's me!

Frosty, Former Snowball

1   Do you know how much easier life was when I was just a
2   snowball? No one expected me to do anything — just sail
3   through the air and occasionally, if the thrower was good, hit
4   some poor kid in the back of the head. Or maybe the face.

5   Life was good. No expectations. No responsibilities. Then
6   here come a bunch of over-zealous kids. They can't just make
7   forts or snow angels — oh no, they gotta build a *man*. A man
8   made out of snow!

9   I get rolled and rolled and rolled and that's when I know
10 something is wrong. There's no way I'm sailing through the air
11 when I'm big as a doghouse!

12 They give me a head and some arms made out of sticks.
13 They think of everything — well, everything but clothes. I got
14 rocks for buttons but no shirt to button up. Go figure.
15 Funniest thing is, I got no clothes, but I got a hat. Kids are
16 strange little creatures, I tell you.

17 So, bam! There I am, alive and moving, and all of a
18 sudden these kids think I'm their new play toy. They want to
19 play games. Climb all over me. Ride my back like a sleigh. I
20 guess they're thinking, "Hey, Mr. Man Made Out of Snow, we
21 made you and that means we *own* you."

22 I was better off being a snowball. All I've been doing is
23 watching the thermometer, praying for it to jump up about ten
24 to twenty degrees. Just let them try riding my back when I'm
25 a puddle!

Ghost-Huntin' Dust Buster

1   *(As if finishing up conducting an interview)* **OK, man.** I think
2 you're going to work out great. We've been so busy lately we
3 just can't keep up. Never knew there were so many ghosts in
4 this town.

5   You understand your duties, right? You're to take this ...
6 *(Pantomimes holding up something.)* Now, I know what you're
7 thinking — it's some kind of reconfigured mini-vac that can
8 suck up ghosts, right? Well, you're absolutely ... *wrong!*
9 That's the *beauty* of it all! This is nothing more than a dust
10 buster, man! Yeah, we added some fancy lights and sounds
11 ... but that's it! It doesn't suck up any ghosts! Heck, it barely
12 sucks up dust!

13   It's amazing what people will believe when they're all
14 creeped-out about some funky noises in their house. See this?
15 *(Pantomimes holding something else up.)* It's the Ghost Stick.
16 You wave it around and close your eyes and after awhile, you
17 push this little button on the end to turn on the lights, and
18 then you're like — "Whoa! There's a spirit in here. Oh, yes. I
19 feel it. It's very strong. And he's angry. Look — the light is
20 turning red ... that's never a good sign."

21   Then you shake your head and mumble to yourself so that
22 they get good and scared. Add in an *"Omigosh"* here and
23 there and they'll be forking over the cash before you know it.
24 It's a sixty-forty split. Got it?

25   Oh, there's one other thing — new guy always has to
26 clean the toilets. Here. *(Pantomimes holding something out.)* You
27 can use the "Ghost Stick."

Stuck-in-a-Rut Snack Man

1   I eat and I eat and I eat. That's all I do. Zooming around
2 looking for food. It's the same thing day after day. Dots, dots,
3 and more dots. There's an occasional strawberry or orange
4 every now and then, but only if I'm fast enough to get one
5 before it disappears. It's a wonder I don't weigh three hundred
6 pounds! But that would be impossible with the amount of
7 running I do.
8   What's the point? Where am I going? I feel like my life is a
9 waste. Like I'm trapped in some sort of maze. It's exhausting.
10 I never get any rest. Stop running, you say? I can't! And if I
11 tell you why, you'll think I'm crazy. But here it is: There are
12 ghosts following me! I don't know if they want the dots or me,
13 but I'm not stopping to find out!
14   If I'm lucky, I find one of these bigger dots — they have
15 some sort of ghost power or something. I eat one and then ...
16 now I know this sounds gross, but remember it's a live-or-die
17 situation ... well, for a few minutes, I can *eat* the ghosts! I get
18 to chase *them* instead of the other way around. And before
19 you get too grossed out, let me tell you, it's like eating air!
20 Believe me, after all the dots I've eaten, I wouldn't mind
21 something a little more meaty!
22   So that's my life ... well, there is one more thing ... but I'm
23 almost afraid to tell you about it. I don't want anything to jinx
24 it. See, every now and then, after I've been running around
25 awhile, there's this girl ... I only get to see her for a few
26 minutes and then she's gone. She's so beautiful. Wears a pink
27 bow in her hair. Has these rosy little cheeks!
28   I don't know how she gets in here, but I can't wait for her
29 to come back! I swear one day I'm going to marry her! She's

1   the only thing that keeps me going. Keeps me running and
2   eating these stupid dots. Maybe today will be the day I get to
3   see her again!

Humpty Dumpty: Assassinated

1   It was all part of a plot. A plot to overthrow the King! I
2 know, because I helped Humpty make the signs. That was
3 part one: Public awareness. We had to let the people know
4 exactly what the King was up to. Budget cuts. Rise in taxes.
5 A new fairy tale tax! We just couldn't let that happen.

6   Humpty knew he could draw the most attention. He was
7 like a walking billboard! It wasn't easy getting him up on that
8 wall. Took me and six other guys, and we were there half the
9 night. But he was up there solid. No way was he coming down
10 until we went and *got* him down.

11   That's why I know he didn't just "fall off" like they're
12 saying. You would've had to pry him off that thing! We had him
13 wedged in good. You can't believe the nonsense you read in
14 the paper! The King *owns* it! Look at this! It's an outrage! All
15 the King's horses and all the King's men couldn't put Humpty
16 together because they weren't there to *help* him! They were
17 there to trample him! That's what horses do!

18   Don't believe me? Then where are the signs? The signs we
19 made to inform the public about what's happening. Did they
20 just disappear into thin air when Humpty "fell" from the wall?
21 No! The King had them destroyed. He didn't want the people
22 reading our propaganda.

23   Fight for your rights, my good people! We mustn't go down
24 without a fight! Rebel in the name of Humpty Dumpty! We
25 cannot let his death be in vain! Long live Humpty! Long live
26 Humpty!

The Not-So-Charming Prince

1   I say you should have the right to do as you wish —
2 especially in your own home! Your own castle! Don't you
3 agree? Well, my parents didn't. Shipped me off to some
4 refining school to learn the do's and don'ts to being a prince.
5 Said I would never find a princess to marry me living the way
6 I do! Well, I say fine! I'll stay a bachelor then! Who wants to
7 act all high and uppity? Like it really matters exactly how I
8 hold a bloomin' teacup! I don't even *like* tea!

9   And if my lady gets offended by a little burp, then too bad
10 for her. Why should I put on any airs! I'm a prince, after all.
11 Most of the fair maidens in town could care less if I were to
12 belch out the alphabet. Which I can do, by the way.

13   Who cares about tying neckties or buffing shoes? Or even
14 picking up my clothes? I have a manservant for those types of
15 things!

16   The funniest part is the courting class. They actually
17 expect me to write these silly love poems to try and win a
18 maiden's hand. Ha! What exactly do we pay the royal poet
19 laureate for? Why would a real man, such as myself, waste
20 time on such drivel?

21   I'll tell you why! I don't have any choice. My parents have
22 threatened to cut me off — take my inheritance — if I don't
23 come back a perfect gentleman. "We want a prince, not a
24 pig," my mother said when she slammed the door to the
25 carriage.

26   Well, fine. A prince they'll get. I'll play their stupid game.
27 Act like the perfect gentleman for the whole world to see. But
28 just you wait, once I'm King of the castle, I'm doing things
29 *my* way!

Chicken Little the Prankster

1   "The sky is falling! The sky is falling!" What morons would
2 believe that? It all started out as a joke, and now everyone's
3 blaming me for their own stupidity. I never dreamed anyone would
4 actually take me seriously! Especially the whole town. Is there no
5 one that has any sense around here? Come on, people, how could
6 the sky possibly fall?

7   It was crazy! Like *War of the Worlds, Part Two*! People jumping
8 out of buildings. Panic and pandemonium everywhere. Looters
9 breaking into buildings. Traffic piled up on the interstate. Does
10 that even make sense? If the sky *was* falling, where were they
11 trying to go?

12   Now I'm stuck in jail with a list of charges against me a mile
13 long. What about them? Shouldn't there be a charge against
14 stupidity? Why is it *my* fault that *everyone* is so gullible?

15   Besides, I only said it to a couple of people. If this "Mayberry
16 town" didn't thrive on gossip, none of this would have happened.
17 But around here, if somebody hiccups, everybody knows it! Within
18 ten minutes the radio was broadcasting for everyone to take cover
19 because the sky was falling!

20   Shouldn't they have checked their facts? Isn't there some
21 kind of regulation they're supposed to follow? The people at the
22 radio and TV stations caused the havoc, not me! And what about
23 that nutcase going around in his car with the megaphone spouting
24 out things about the "end of the world!" Why didn't *he* get
25 arrested?

26   There's been an injustice here! An injustice against the
27 innocent! Where are the newscasters now? Doesn't anybody want
28 to hear my side of the story?

Bachelor Beast

1   Everything was just fine until *she* came along! I had things
2   the way I liked it. I dressed the way *I* wanted, ate what *I*
3   wanted, and did what *I* wanted. Everything was my way. Best
4   of all, *I* was in charge of the remote! In other words, even
5   though I was only a Prince, I was the King of this castle.

6   Then in stumbles this chick trying to find her father. How
7   was I to know the man was hiding out in my cellar? I tell them
8   both to *go*! Get out!

9   *(Mimicking a girl)* "No! I will pay my father's debt. Take me
10 instead."

11   What debt? Her father didn't owe me anything! I just
12 wanted them both out of my hair. Out of my castle. But she
13 wouldn't leave. Absolutely refused. I'm pretty sure she took
14 one look around and decided she'd found her sugar daddy! It's
15 obvious she'd been living in poverty — she had on the most
16 wretched dress!

17   I've tried everything to get her to leave! I've locked her in
18 her room, yelled and screamed at her, even begged her to
19 leave! Some nights I've refused to give her any dinner!
20 Nothing works. She'll go about the castle singing and talking
21 to the servants — I think she's turning them against me! I
22 know they must be slipping her food. And they've shown her
23 the library — *my* library! Now I can't get her out of it. I have
24 to go to the bathroom if I want to read in peace!

25   *(Pause)* I guess it's not all bad. She is *kind of* pretty to
26 look at. And she does have a pretty voice. Sometimes she
27 wears this perfume that smells really nice ... maybe I could try
28 harder to get along with her ...

29   *(Whiny)* But she wants me to take a bath. And wear a

1   suit. And use a fork. The absolute worst one is, she wants me
2   to *cut my hair*! Oh, who am I kidding? No girl in the kingdom
3   is worth that!

Cupid Cares Less

1   Why do I even bother? They just mess it up. Oh, sure, they
2   start out all googly-eyed and dreamy-looking, promising the
3   moon and stars, making everlasting vows ... that last about two
4   minutes! I mean really, have you seen what the divorce rate is?
5   Why do people even say the "L" word? They don't mean it!
6   What they really mean to say is, "I care about you this second,
7   and I might even care about you in the next few seconds, but
8   make me mad *one time*, and I'm outta here!"
9   When did commitment fall out of the love pact? When did
10 love become so meaningless? It's made a mockery of my job.
11 Made me into a laughingstock. No one believes in the power of
12 love anymore. It's a joke!
13 I might as well be shooting poison arrows! Everything
14 becomes bitter after awhile anyhow. The loving touch becomes
15 careless. The dreamy look becomes disgusted. The spark
16 between two lovers becomes a dagger. Nothing is sacred!
17 I do all the work in the beginning, and nobody does any
18 work after! It's like they just *expect* things to stay the way they
19 were without putting any effort into it! Do they think I can just
20 hang out in their lives forever, making sure they stay in love?
21 You know what love is? Love is ... for *losers*. Love is ... for
22 the *dogs*. Love is ... blind ... what am I saying? Love isn't *blind*;
23 it sees every little annoying thing! And then it blows it up into
24 a really *big* thing! And then it stomps on every shred of love
25 there is until there's nothing left *to* love! Well, all you lovers out
26 there — guess what? You're on your *own*! I am *done with love*!

Hunchback of a Picky Dame

1   Just be friends? Is she freakin' kidding me? I saved this
2   chick's life — risked my own safety to help her, and *this* is the
3   thanks I get? A brother-like kiss on the cheek and a pat on
4   my hunched-over back? What the heck is up with that? Can't
5   she see how much I love her? How well I'd take care of her?
6   Of course not. All she cares about is her precious prince. But
7   did he do anything to save her?

8   No! He practically ran like a little girl when the fire started!
9   If I'd known she was going to turn on me like this, I might've
10 left them both in there. Instead, like the idiot the town thinks
11 I am, I save not only her — *but him too*! What was I thinking?
12 Maybe if he hadn't gotten out, I would've at least had a
13 chance. Now all she can think of is living happily ever after
14 with hunk-face over there.

15 Oh, he looks good now, even *I'll* admit that. But what
16 about in the years to come? Is he going to be so handsome
17 when those wavy locks start to recede? When Mr. Blondie
18 becomes Mr. Baldy? She'll dump him faster than she dumped
19 me!

20 I don't know who's more shallow, her or him! Normally a
21 prince wouldn't even look twice at a trashy gypsy girl like her.
22 She wouldn't be good enough to shine his boots! But he took
23 one look at that face — and those hips — and he was drooling
24 more than his oversized horse! I'm surprised he even saw her
25 in the first place. He was so busy checking out his reflection
26 in the window that he practically ran her over!

27 Well Mr. and Mrs. Shallow can have each other. As far as
28 being friends, no way! With a friend like her, who'd need
29 enemies?

From Zero to Zorro

1   Kids can be cruel. Yeah, I know everybody knows that.
2 Everybody gets teased a little every now and then. But then
3 comes the nickname that sticks. The one that everyone
4 remembers. And that's it. For the rest of your life.

5   Just because of a stupid football game back in middle
6 school. We got creamed fifty-one to zero. Skunked. Bad. The
7 whole team was responsible though, right? Wrong. The
8 quarterback got all the blame. The quarterback who, just the
9 game before, scored forty-five points and won the game. That
10 same quarterback — me — went from hero to zero in that one
11 cold, wet afternoon.

12   Lost the game. Lost my girlfriend. Lost the team spirit.
13 Everything. I was the school loser.

14   I had to do something. I couldn't even show my face any
15 more — hence, the mask. I didn't want anyone to recognize
16 me. Funny, though, how a little thing like that changes a
17 person. Not only did people see me differently, I saw myself
18 differently. Mysterious. Dangerous. I started doing things I'd
19 never dreamed of doing. Taking risks that no man would dare
20 to take — much less a teenage boy.

21   It took awhile for word to get around. At first there were a
22 lot of whispers and rumors. No one knew the masked man
23 was me. By day I was Zero. By night — the magnificent Zorro.
24 I became notorious. Celebrated. The mystery of a lifetime.

25   It no longer mattered what anyone thought of me. Or what
26 horrible nickname they called me. I was Zorro, the masked
27 man of the night.

Big Feet + Hairy Back = No Girl

1   Big feet are the least of my problems. In fact, you might
2   call them my one and only asset. After all, you know what
3   they say about a guy and the size of his feet — well, I won't
4   go into *that*. Besides, that'll never be an issue for me! I can't
5   get a girl to come within ten feet of me!

6   It's the hair that's the problem. It's everywhere! I look like
7   a freakin' ape! It pokes out from under my collar, from under
8   my sleeves. Even my feet are covered in funky fur, right down
9   to my toes!

10 I've tried everything. Shaving. Hair removal creams.
11 Waxing. Do you *know* how bad that hurts? I could only stand
12 to get one strip done! I practically passed out from the pain!
13 Then it looked like a tire track running up my back. And the
14 hair grew back thicker than ever.

15 I know they've got pills to grow your hair. What about
16 something to make the darn stuff fall out? I'd gladly go bald
17 if I could drop a couple pounds of hair off this body!

18 Do you have any idea how hot I get under all this? It's like
19 wearing a fur coat all year long. I swear I don't know how dogs
20 do it. No wonder they pant all of the time!

21 And speaking of dogs — you know that great wet dog
22 smell? It's killer isn't it? Well, multiply that by a thousand, and
23 that's me! Sometimes I make *myself* nauseous! And if that
24 doesn't do it — finding food stuck in the hair on my face sure
25 does. I'm like the nastiest man on earth!

26 So now you know the truth about me. The legend of Big
27 Foot. Do yourself a *big* favor and leave me alone. Believe me,
28 you'll be glad you did!

Disillusioned Sandman

1   This job is *nothing* like I thought it would be. It doesn't have
2 the first thing to do with sand — not the real kind anyway! I
3 pictured sandy beaches. Girls in hot bikinis. Drinks with fancy
4 umbrellas. Parties and bonfires. Girls gone wild. The kind of job
5 any guy would dream of having!

6   Ha! You know what? This stupid job has *zero* to do with any
7 of that. I've been working here a week and I've *yet* to see a
8 beach. In fact, I don't get to see anything at all. I work in
9 complete darkness — stuck on the stinking third shift! I haven't
10 seen the light of day since I started working. I'd quit, but I'm too
11 tired to go job hunting!

12   Who ever heard of a Sandman that helps people sleep?
13 Whatever happened to counting sheep or drinking warm milk?
14 Or Tylenol P.M. — that stuff is the bomb! Take one blue pill and
15 sleep like a baby. What the heck do people need *me* for?

16   And if they *do* need me — then what about the hot chicks
17 wanting to nap at the beach? Why can't I help them? How does
18 a guy get promoted to a job like that?

19   I'm stuck on the worst shift. You'd think I'd at least get to
20 see girls in their pj's! You know, as a perk — but *no*! No one
21 and I mean *no one* — above the age of fifteen and under the age
22 of forty *ever* sleeps with a light on. Not even a tiny one. It's pitch
23 black the whole night. And if you get caught flashing — that's
24 code for turning on the light — it's instant termination!
25 Absolutely *no* peeking allowed!

26   I don't know how much more I can take. How can they
27 expect any normal guy to work this way? I think it's time I talked
28 to the boss. I'm not a bad employee. I just got the wrong job.
29 If he'd just put me on the *day shift*, I wouldn't *have* to peek!

Billy the **Man**

1   Geez, what's a guy gotta do around here to be called a man?
2 I've wrangled horses, had my fair share of pretty women, and
3 been called an outlaw since I was twelve. I've broken out of jail
4 more times than I can count and escaped death by hearing the
5 slow breeze of a bullet passing my ear!
6   But if that ain't enough to convince you I ain't no kid, how
7 about the fact that I've killed me almost two dozen men! Some
8 of 'em 'cause they was trying to get me first. And some of 'em
9 just 'cause I didn't like the way they looked.
10   That sound like a kid to you? I know I'm kind of on the short
11 side for a bandit — only stand five-foot-eight — and I weigh a
12 mere hundred and forty pounds. But I think I've proven that size
13 don't matter a bit when it comes to being a legend. What's it
14 gonna take for people to stop calling me "Billy the Kid"? I may
15 have been a young 'un when I started — but come on folks, that
16 was almost ten years ago!
17   I've been taking care of business since my mother died when
18 I was only thirteen. Don't that count for nothing? I never even
19 knew my good-for-nothing father. Me and my brother was forced
20 to live in foster care. In separate homes. That sure grows a kid
21 up fast. Having no family left to take care of you. Even when I
22 should've been a kid, I wasn't. I've been a man long before I even
23 had peach fuzz on my chin.
24   I think it's high time I earned a little respect. I've been the
25 quickest horse thief this side of Arizona. The fastest draw
26 around. Can beat just about anyone in poker. Shoot any target
27 plumb out of the sky. I guess if these idiots they call "Sheriff" are
28 ever smart — or quick — enough to catch me, I'll have to set
29 them straight. They've picked the wrong man to call a "kid."

Piggy Pen's Phobia

1   I know everyone's talking about me. Spreading rumors
2 about how I stink and don't even shower after gym class. I
3 guess in a way they're not really rumors though, 'cause it's
4 true. I don't shower here at school. But it's not like I don't
5 have good reasons!

6   The showers here are *so* gross! There's mold in every line
7 of grout, and who knows what kind of fungus is growing in
8 those stalls! I'd have to take a shower *after* my shower just
9 to get the funk from the floor off my feet! It's absolutely
10 disgusting.

11   And who ever came up with the idea of community
12 showers? What moron thought that it would be OK for a
13 bunch of guys to get naked together? I'm not about to stand
14 there — exposed — for the whole room to see! It's not like I'm
15 ashamed or anything — 'cause I'm not! I'm just very private.
16 Besides, how do I know who's looking at me when my back is
17 turned? I don't know these guys that well. In fact, there's *no*
18 guy I ever want to know well enough to be naked around. Isn't
19 that what we *all* should want? I mean, if it were a room full of
20 girls — maybe!

21   If getting naked isn't bad enough, the whole towel-
22 whipping thing is enough to keep me in my clothes. I've seen
23 the red welts those guys leave on each other. Why would I
24 want to be a part of that? They're like a bunch of animals.
25 They even hold each other down — never mind the body parts
26 flying all over the place! And no one even seems to care!

27   Well, I do. I'm not running around a locker room naked
28 while guys chase me trying to prove who's top towel whipper.
29 So, yeah. I may be a little "ripe" after gym class. They can

1   call me "piggy pen" all they want. I'll take my showers in the

2   safety of my own home — thank you very much!

Kasper the Seeing Ghost

1   I see dead people. Ha ha! Of course I do! I'm a ghost, that's
2   who I'm supposed to see. The weird thing is that I see *live*
3   people, too. And they can see me! It's really quite scary.   I
4   thought I'd get to live in this house in peace. No one would
5   bother me, and I wouldn't bother them back. But *no*! Now that
6   they've seen me they won't leave me alone.

7   And they bring their friends, too. It's like I'm the major
8   attraction around here. I can't get a minute to myself. They're
9   always putting their hands through me — for some reason they
10   think that's really cool. Like some kind of magic trick or
11   something. Hello, people! I'm made of air — putting your hand
12   through me is *not* rocket science! Put your hand through a wall
13   — now that would be impressive.

14   They want to know about their dead friends, too. Like just
15   because *I'm* dead I'm supposed to know *everyone* that's dead.
16   Do they have any idea how many dead people there are? It's like
17   saying just 'cause you live in Texas, you should know every
18   Texan!

19   Sometimes I make stuff up just to freak them out. "Yeah. I
20   saw Joe the other night. He says he hates your hair that color.
21   He thinks purple would be really cool." You should see their
22   faces! Sometimes they even do the stupid things I tell them. It
23   almost makes it all worthwhile. *Almost.*

24   I just wish these stupid *alive* people would leave me alone.
25   Can't they leave me in this dimension I seem to be stuck in and
26   go on with their lives? Go on with their hamburger-, french-fries-,
27   and pizza-eating lives! Watching them eat those things is killing
28   me — well, it would be killing me — if I wasn't *dead* already!
29   Give the ghost a break, folks, and find another freak show!

Larry Plotter,
Ophthalmologist Wannabe

1   It was a stupid thing to do. I see that now — ha ha.
2   Actually I'm lucky that I can *see* anything! Thank goodness
3   my aim is bad, or I might have lost an eye! Instead I've got
4   this stupid lightning bolt scar that everyone thinks is some
5   kind of war wound caused by "He Who Should Not be
6   Named." If only they knew! I'd be the laughingstock of
7   Bogwarts instead of some kind of hero.

8   I still think if I had a shorter wand it might've worked. It
9   was just too powerful that close to my face. I still can't
10   believe it didn't work, though. It seemed like such a simple
11   procedure. Zip, zip, and it'd be done. Instant laser surgery.
12   Twenty-twenty vision. No more dorky glasses. Never a need for
13   scratchy contacts.

14   I was even thinking that if my surgery went well enough, I
15   could make a little cash on the side. I could let Rob be my
16   assistant since he never has any money. There wouldn't be a
17   wizard here wearing glasses!

18   Best thing is I'd finally be better than Harmony at
19   something. She's always so cocky about being the first to
20   know everything about spell making. She'd be so jealous that
21   she hadn't thought of it herself. Next thing you know, she'd be
22   doing cosmetic surgery with her wand — wart and freckle
23   remover — or something lame like that! But everyone would
24   know that she stole the idea from me!

25   Yeah. It would've been so nice ... had it worked. Maybe I
26   need more distance. I don't want to scar the rest of my face,
27   after all! I need to practice on someone — or something! Hey,
28   I wonder if any of the creatures in the forest have vision
29   problems!

Chuckie from the Chocolate Factory — Six Months Later

1   This place is killing me! I'm serious. I knew winning the
2 chocolate factory from Mr. Willie was going to change my life,
3 but I didn't think it was going to *claim* it! Do you know how
4 many hours I have to put in around here? Seems like no one
5 can make a decision for themselves! I have to oversee
6 everything. Every stinking thing has to be approved by me!

7   The worst part is, I can't spend a minute in my office
8 either, 'cause if I turn my back on those lazy little workers,
9 they think it's instant break time! I'm out in the factory all day
10 long and doing paperwork at my desk *all night long*! I haven't
11 been outside since I got here. And I'm in serious need of some
12 fresh air! I never thought it could happen — but yes, folks, you
13 *can* get sick of the smell of freshly churned chocolate — trust
14 me! I may never eat another chocolate bar for as long as I live,
15 which may not be that long anyway! At this rate, I'm headed
16 for an early grave!

17   I'll admit that it was cool at first. That golden ticket was
18 better than winning the lottery. And then, Mr. Willie signing
19 over his company to me — well, it was crazy to say the least!
20 All of a sudden, I was the most popular kid in the world. I had
21 friends and "relatives" coming out of the woodwork! It was
22 awesome until I realized that no one really cared about *me*;
23 they were lining up for either a job, or — more likely — a
24 handout! Everybody wanted a piece of the action.

25   I thought owning a chocolate factory would keep me a kid
26 forever. Ha! Besides, I don't *own* the factory, it owns *me*!
27 Work, bills, taxes, employee benefits, union meetings ... who
28 can keep up with all that?

29   I know it's weird, but I wish I'd never found that golden

1 ticket! I miss my crooked old house with the leaky roof and
2 creaky boards ... and my grandparents who used to sleep on
3 the bed in the living room. We might have been dirt poor, but
4 man, were we happy!

The Extraterrestrial

1   They don't call this the blue marble planet for nothing, I
2   can tell you that! And you want to know why? 'Cause the
3   people here must have marbles for brains! I've been to some
4   pretty undeveloped planets before, but this one takes the
5   cake!

6   What have they been doing for the past hundred years?
7   Watching television? That's *so* last millennium! Who's in
8   charge of technology around here? Teletubbies? I've been here
9   two days already and have *yet* to get even one bar of reception
10 on my cellphone! No matter where I go! Upstairs. Downstairs.
11 Out in a field. How can anyone function with poor reception
12 like this? The one time I made it through to my ship, the call
13 dropped before I had a chance to give my coordinates! Then
14 it kept saying "system busy." Busy doing what? Not placing
15 my call, that's for sure!

16 I was looking around this kid's room and I thought I'd
17 found a receiver ... it was some sort of white pod thing ... but
18 when I flipped it on, some really strange sounding *music* came
19 out! I tried yelling to the people on the other end, but how
20 could anyone possibly hear me over all that racket? You can't
21 communicate with a piece of equipment like that! What a
22 waste of radio waves! It's like these earthlings *want* to be cut
23 off from each other.

24 My best bet is to head for the mountains ... maybe if I get
25 high enough up I can get some sort of reception. If all else
26 fails, I'll send smoke signals! Anything to get me out of here!

Advice from King Wrong

1   It was the blue eyes that got me. The way they looked like
2 little blue ponds. The blonde wavy hair didn't help, either. All
3 I'd ever seen before was dark skin, dark hair — which is great,
4 don't get me wrong — but variety is the spice of life, right? So
5 you can imagine how surprised I was to see her tied up there.

6   I guess if I'm being totally honest, though, it was the hot
7 white dress she *barely* had on that was the real clincher. With
8 the fire going on behind her, I could practically see right
9 through it.

10   So I took her. Thought maybe I'd keep her as a plaything.
11 Took her back to my place — but let me tell you something
12 you won't believe — I wish I'd left her tied to that tree. I do!
13 That broad wouldn't stop screaming! I tried to nudge her a
14 little to get her to shut up, and she screamed even louder.
15 Man, did she have a set of pipes on her. I never knew my head
16 could hurt so bad.

17   Then, because of *her*, I got trapped, caged, and brought to
18 some big lit-up city where they displayed me like a trophy for
19 the whole darn world to see. Now I got all kinds of people
20 screaming at me.

21   But that's not even the worst of it! To beat it all, I'm stuck
22 on the top of this building — airplanes buzzing around my
23 head like pesky flies — and guess what else? The beautiful
24 blonde girl followed me up here, and *she's still screaming*!

25   I think I'm going to jump just to get away from her. So,
26 you guys take my advice, there ain't no chick — no matter
27 how blue her eyes or how see-through her dress — worth this
28 kind of trouble!

Robbin' the Woods

1   *(With a mobster accent, if possible)* **OK**, so here's the way it's
2   gonna go down. There's gonna be a little old lady coming
3   through here in about fifteen minutes. Weekly grocery run.
4   Cashes her government check after she shops. Rodney here's
5   gonna jump her and you're gonna grab her bag. Then you run
6   it over here to me. We'll split the loot fifty-fifty. Fifty for you's
7   guys and fifty for me.

8   Oh, wait. I forgot about the blasted poor. We gotta give
9   something back — you know, create a little good will and all.
10 So here's what we're gonna do. I'm gonna give you twenty
11 percent, and you twenty percent, and the poor ten percent. I'll
12 make do with what's left. You guys can spare a mere ten
13 percent, can't ya? For the good of the cause?

14 I thought so. Now, if you get caught, you've never seen
15 me, right? 'Cause you know I know where you live. And where
16 your family lives. And accidents happen out here in the forest.
17 You know that, right? But we ain't gonna worry ourselves
18 about that now, are we? 'Cause you guys are my men! And
19 we're like family, right? And nobody turns their back on their
20 own family, right?

21 Look — here she comes! Steady. Don't rush it. She might
22 have a frying pan or something. OK. *Go!* And make sure you
23 grab that cane! It's probably worth something!

About the Author

This is Rebecca North Young's second book of monologs. Writing *Famous Fantasy Character Monologs* was particularly exciting because Rebecca has always been enchanted with fairy tale characters. She remembers rewriting the tale of Cinderella as "Asherella" when she was in elementary school. The assignment called for a two-minute play. Rebecca's was well over ten minutes by the time she finished writing it! She got an "A" even though the teacher made her cut it short!

Rebecca also enjoys directing drama for her church. Over the past few years, she has written and directed numerous plays for middle- and high-school students. She co-founded a drama group called One Voice which travels annually to perform at various churches. Her great passion is combining writing, drama, and working with youth.

Rebecca currently works as a technical trainer in Lexington, Kentucky. She has a B.A. in Communications/Marketing from the University of Kentucky.

Rebecca moved from upstate New York when she was eleven years old and has called Kentucky home ever since. She lives with her husband (Frank), three daughters (Heather, Kristina, and Ashley), and two cats (who have names but are more often than not called Orange Kitty and Gray Kitty). Besides writing fiction, plays, monologs, and picture books, Rebecca enjoys reading, scrapbooking, hiking, and spending time with her awesome girls.

Her favorite quote is "You aren't finished when you lose, you're finished when you quit."

Order Form

Meriwether Publishing Ltd.
PO Box 7710
Colorado Springs CO 80933-7710
Phone: 800-937-5297 Fax: 719-594-9916
Website: www.meriwether.com

Please send me the following books:

_____	**Famous Fantasy Character Monologs** **#BK-B286**	**$15.95**
	by Rebecca Young	
	Starring the Not-So-Wicked Witch and more	
_____	**100 Great Monologs #BK-B276**	**$15.95**
	by Rebecca Young	
	A collection of monologs, duologs and triologs for actors	
_____	**Winning Monologs for Young Actors** **#BK-B127**	**$15.95**
	by Peg Kehret	
	Honest-to-life monologs for young actors	
_____	**50 Great Monologs for Student Actors** **#BK-B197**	**$14.95**
	by Bill Majeski	
	A workbook of comedy characterizations for students	
_____	**The Flip Side #BK-B221**	**$15.95**
	by Heather H. Henderson	
	64 point-of-view monologs for teens	
_____	**Audition Monologs for Student Actors** **#BK-B232**	**$15.95**
	edited by Roger Ellis	
	Selections from contemporary plays	
_____	**Young Women's Monologs from** **Contemporary Plays #BK-B272**	**$15.95**
	edited by Gerald Lee Ratliff	
	Professional auditions for aspiring actresses	

These and other fine Meriwether Publishing books are available at your local bookstore or direct from the publisher. Prices subject to change without notice. Check our website or call for current prices.

Name: _____ e-mail: _____

Organization name: _____

Address: _____

City: _____ State: _____

Zip: _____ Phone: _____

❑ **Check enclosed**

❑ **Visa / MasterCard / Discover #** _____

Signature: _____ *Expiration date:* _____
(required for credit card orders)

Colorado residents: Please add 3% sales tax.
Shipping: Include $3.95 for the first book and 75¢ for each additional book ordered.

❑ *Please send me a copy of your complete catalog of books and plays.*